DAVID QUANTICK

The DANGEROUS Book

FOR MIDDLE-AGED MEN

A MANUAL FOR MANAGING
THE MID-LIFE CRISIS

preface
publishing

Published by Preface 2009

10 9 8 7 6 5 4 3 2 1

Copyright © David Quantick, 2009

David Quantick has asserted his right to be identified as the author of this
work under the Copyright, Designs and Patents Act 1988

All photographs © Hulton/Getty Archival

First published in Great Britain in 2009 by Preface Publishing
20 Vauxhall Bridge Road
London SW1V 2SA

An imprint of The Random House Group Limited

www.rbooks.co.uk
www.prefacepublishing.co.uk

Addresses for companies within The Random House Group Limited
can be found at www.randomhouse.co.uk

The Random House Group Limited Reg. No. 954009

A CIP catalogue record for this book is available from the British Library

ISBN 978 1 84809 200 6

The Random House Group Limited supports The Forest Stewardship
Council (FSC), the leading international forest certification organisation.
All our titles that are printed on Greenpeace-approved FSC-certified paper
carry the FSC logo. Our paper procurement policy can be found at
www.rbooks.co.uk/environment

Mixed Sources
Product group from well-managed
forests and other controlled sources
www.fsc.org Cert no. TT-COC-2139
© 1996 Forest Stewardship Council
FSC

Designed and typeset in Bodoni Old Face by Peter Ward
Printed and bound in Great Britain by Clays Ltd St Ives PLC

For Andy and Fiona, who have put up with my dangerous middle age for about 20 years now, and Junior and Nell, who will have to put up with it for the next 20 . . .

CONTENTS

Introduction
ix

INTRODUCTION

*'The lime-green Vauxhall Zafira swerved on a sixpence
to narrowly avoid the three heat-seeking ground-to-air
missiles, its tyres squealing over the neat tarmac of Acacia
Gardens as it executed a perfect U-turn into the
small driveway of number 32 . . .'*

We all dream of living life dangerously, but we can't all be
international assassins or dangerous super-spies. Or so we are
told. There is surely more to life than the ordinary; and there
is also surely no real reason why the fantasies of our child-
hood, our adolescence and, if we're completely honest, our
20s and 30s, shouldn't at least try and come true.

This, at least, is the thinking behind this book. This is the
philosophy that fires *The Dangerous Book For Middle-Aged Men.*

*' . . . Bond instinctively disengaged the child locks. 'Keep
your heads down, kids, and run like hell,' he snapped, and
the two children, a flurry of school bags and rumpled
uniforms, obediently sped toward the front door, silhouetted
by the fireball that had engulfed the conservatory extension
at number 34, its flames billowing perilously close to the
potting shed where Mr Norris kept his prized Atco Royale
sit-on lawnmower and its three tidily stacked canisters of
two-stroke petrol . . .'*

Middle age used to be a time to sit back on your burst sofa,
tap out your aged pipe and settle in for those ever-so-slightly
bleak years between marriage and retirement. The term
'middle-aged' has been a kind of insult for so long that we
forget it's only a description. Being a middle-aged man is no

bar to being an exciting – even a Dangerous – man. Look at everyone from Iggy Pop to Captain Scott, from Richard Hammond to Johnny Rotten. These people did not and have not and *will not* let middle age wither them nor custom stale their infinite dangerousness.

And now, thanks to *The Dangerous Book for Middle-Aged Men*, you can join them.

> *'. . . Bond flung open the driver's door and creased his eyes in pain. 'Agh, my back,' he winced, as his seat belt relinquished its firm hold of his manly paunch and spun back into its socket. Instinctively he flung himself from the vehicle just at its windscreen erupted in a hailstorm of glass. He careered over the box hedge and onto the garden patio, bullets scything past his ears like angry mosquitoes . . .'*

Maybe you're suffering a mid-life crisis. Maybe you feel that growing old gracefully is all right for Nelson Mandela and Her Majesty the Queen but right now you're not interested. You are only middle-aged once and the world, if not entirely your oyster, still has lots of oystery bits left in it. If so, then *The Dangerous Book for Middle-Aged Men* is the book for you. It's the mid-life manual, the not-yet-anywhere-near-geriatric guidebook. More SAS than Saga, this book will tell you how to live life to the full, and how to do so dangerously.

> *'With one final energy-sapping leap he hurled himself upon the pink Lazytown tricycle which propelled him, torpedo-like, to the open front door. 'It's for you,' said a stern-looking woman in early middle age, a portable telephone in her outstretched hand. 'Hello . . . Bond speaking . . . Yes, Tim Bond . . . I see . . . So you'll be coming to fix the boiler on Wednesday . . . You'd better.*

> *Or what? Or you'll be trying to pull that spanner out*
> *from a place you don't normally find spanners, that's*
> *what.' Bond put the phone down. A smile played on his*
> *lips. A dangerous smile . . .'*

Dreams can become real. The ordinary can be extraordinary. And, with a few hints from this book, YOU can become DANGEROUS!

Now read on . . .

CHAPTER 1

DANGEROUSLY BORED

There comes a point in the life of many British human males when the monotony and/or disappointment of their jobs, relationships or existence makes it increasingly difficult for them to maintain their own image of themselves as a sexually irresistible secret service agent who is licensed to kill. That's what they want you to think, anyway. In actual fact, boredom in the right hands can be both a dangerous weapon and a powerful tool for change.

Consider this: in the East people spend years (and charge lots of money for) teaching and learning how to do nothing at all. They actually train themselves to look at a wall for hours. They are skilled in sitting on the same spot for ages, emptying their minds of all practical thought. They call it 'Zen Buddhism', or 'transcendental meditation'. They say they are achieving 'trance states' and 'nirvana'. And yet, in the West, when we sit in the office or on the train or in the doctor's waiting room doing *exactly* the same thing we call it 'boredom'.

Clearly we need to redefine our terms here. Because when some Zen master in China or India has been staring at the wall for six hours he doesn't get up and go to the loo for a crafty fag. No, he splits a block of wood in two with his bare palm. He does a bit of levitating. He unlocks the secrets of the material universe. There's got to be something in this; your Buddhist positively relishes what we call boredom because it seems that by tuning out from his existence – or, as we would say, 'not doing any work' – he is able to lift himself onto a different plane and become a kind of superman. So we here at *The Dangerous Book* propose a new, exciting way of dealing with boredom – put your ennui to good use, and welcome to the world of Zen Boredom, the riskiest, most exciting form of boredom there is.

Zen Boredom (@ *Dangerous Book For Middle-Aged Men*) is a far from ancient discipline which takes the best of Buddhism, Transcendental Meditation and all the stuff the old bloke in Kung Fu on telly in the 1970s told David Carradine and applies it to modern life. Zen Boredom says, next time you're in the office, staring at a Garfield calendar on the far wall for the 78th time and trying to remember if you've had lunch or if you just wish it was lunchtime, let your mind drift. Let it settle on some striking thought – how you might be able to get away with offing your co-workers, or perhaps how with one keystroke you could hack into the wages department and increase your salary by a million pounds. Let your mind walk free as your body prepares to harden itself and decapitate Skinner from the third floor with one slice of your Zen hand.

Of course, as with all great disciplines of the mind, Zen Boredom has to be mastered properly before it can be tested. Otherwise, as you approach the threshold of truly enlightened dullness one false move might mean that instead of becoming a finely honed mind warrior you might just go mad from boredom and spend the rest of your working life sitting in the corner by the photocopier, rocking slightly and moaning. Then again, this is considered normal behaviour in most offices, so no real loss frankly.

CHAPTER 2

DANGEROUS CAREERS

At this time in your life – the midpoint – you are like the bubble on a spirit level. Halfway along, the pressure is on you to maintain some kind of balance and not go frothing up and down like a pint of lager balanced on a clown's head. You are naturally inclined to rebel against this; who wouldn't be? Look at your job. It's awful, isn't it? It pays just enough to cover your mortgage and your debts. It's no fun whatsoever, and you suspect deep down that you're probably not very good at it. Your colleagues either patronise you or despise you, you have to wear a tie, and the local sandwich shop is revolting. And here you are, midpoint, six inches along the ruler of life. Why not just walk out the door? 'Stick your rotten job,' you say to the boss as you throw your tie in the bin and walk out with your head held high, cheered to the roof by your chastened male colleagues and kissed by your now unusually beautiful female colleagues.

It's not going to be like that, though, is it? Most likely the boss will be out, so you'll have to go and see his assistant who's a jumped-up little twerp earning five times what you do because he went to Oxbridge and you'll get nervous and he won't hear you saying 'Stick your rotten job,' so you'll have to repeat it, which will make you feel foolish, and the whole thing will take place inside a glass-walled office, so instead of your colleagues hearing your clarion call of departure they'll just see a jumped-up little twerp soundlessly laughing at you, and when you come out everyone will assume that in fact you've been sacked, and they won't be surprised.

Nevertheless, we do sympathise. If you're reading this, chances are you feel you have to do something, and we have options to suggest; but remember that, like the bubble in the spirit level, too much displacement and you'll just explode in a little cloud of whatever they make the bubbles in spirit levels from. So, while this is a book devoted to finding ways of adding Danger to your life, we are bound to advise you that, like mortgage rates and indeed bubbles in spirit levels, your good luck can go down as well as up. Maybe you don't even need to actually leave work – maybe you can be Dangerous from within. Mao said the revolutionary moves among the people like a fish moves through water, but then it was his water. Subvert! Disrupt! Attack! Be Dangerous!

MAKING THE BOSS LOOK A FOOL

The boss is a fool. This is a given. Male, female, young, old, French – it doesn't matter, all bosses are fools. They may have made the company fifty million pounds more than last year and you may have caused several factories to close – so what? The boss is still a fool. And this can be exploited. Any decision the boss makes will have consequences; every action has an equal and opposite reaction, and if the office has made enormous profits thanks to your boss, then somewhere else someone is suffering. When the new figures go up, bring in that DVD of children in South-East Asia being forced at gunpoint to make products similar to yours. Several of the younger women in the office will cry and the tea ladies will look askance at the boss. If he rewards a worker with promotion, hint strongly that this was done to destroy a co-worker who's been waiting for a better job since 1990. Never mind that said co-worker can barely work the lavatory, let alone run a department: pretty soon the boss will be seen as a harsh crusher of souls.

Keep this up and one day you will be the boss, and everyone will hate *you*. Excellent . . .

BEING KICKED UPSTAIRS

Or The Foreman Ploy. If you're not so much really bad at your job as just a pain in the arse who nobody likes, it can be difficult in these litigious times for an employer to actually sack you. Use this fact. Try and cut down on all the things you do which might actually lead to a sacking – the best way to do this is to stop working altogether – and concentrate on honing the aspects of your personality which people really dislike. Soon people won't care what happens to you so long as you just go away. You are now in a position, amazingly, to demand a better job with more pay – only in a different office. Try for one by the sea, because maybe you'll buy a yacht now.

SHIFTING THE BLAME

Of course it was you who cocked up. So what? It's always going to be somebody, isn't it? And at least when it's you, that means you've got some idea of what's going on. In a way, your incompetence has allowed you to control the situation. So long as nobody else finds out that you've lost an account/ insulted a new client/flooded Dundee, then you are the master. Use this strange new undeserved power while you can. Lay a trap for a rival. Spread rumours that in his last job he lost accounts/insulted clients/flooded large Scottish towns. Then, when news gets out he or she will get the blame because they 'did the same thing at their last place of work'.

Oops!

DISRUPTION

If it looks like you're making a mess of things, your role model here is the idiot rogue trader Nick Leeson: the best way out is to *really* make a mess of things. Instead of just getting a few numbers crunched wrongly, get into the accounts computer and chew things up like a starving dog with a copy of the *Sunday Times*. Don't stop at being inept on the phone, deliberately insult some suppliers. Order things that the company doesn't even understand, let alone need. Get in a couple of tons of cold-fusion components. Buy a Fabergé egg. Introduce cats into the ventilation system. Celebrate Canada Day by giving the company to some Canadians you met online. The possibilities are endless.

GETTING SACKED IN A GOOD WAY

There are very few good ways of getting sacked. Anything involving nudity, for example, is always bad. Death and physical injury also will not look good at any future job interview. Even incompetence, however much it may be an essential part of the daily office grind, is frowned upon and won't get you a good reference (although see GETTING KICKED UPSTAIRS). So if all else fails, and you are going to leave your job in an involuntary fashion, make sure you go out the way you want to go out. This may require some preparation. It's no good just shouting 'You can't fire me! I quit!' because the boss will just say 'No, I fired you. You can't just say it and then it's true.' Similarly, walking out of his office grinning and making thumbs-up gestures is unlikely to fool anyone either. You need a plan.

Before you get sacked – and it shouldn't come out of the blue, people are always getting sacked, even competent people – establish a backstory. Create a file on your desktop called WHISTLEBLOWER! and cover it with your hand when people walk past, so they'll be bound to come back later and look at it. Pretend you're phoning *Panorama* or *Newsnight* with information about your employer. Say 'Not for long' whenever the boss makes a statement about what the company is doing (this is always good, by the way, as it makes you look like you know something, and might actually worry the boss). This way, when you do get the heave-ho you can give your former co-workers the impression that you were working on a big exposé of the company and you have been scapegoated.

PRETENDING YOU'VE NOT BEEN SACKED

Ordinarily this is a rather drab refusal to admit failure and conjures up images of a man in a sitcom saying goodbye to his wife and going to the park to eat sandwiches from his briefcase. If this is the plan that appeals to you, make it a bit more Dangerous. Don't go to 'work' in your usual suit. Dress as D'Artagnan and claim you've been asked to join The Three Musketeers. When you leave the house, put on a false moustache, come home and attempt to seduce your own wife. Spend your savings on a sandwich board and parade up and down outside the office claiming that 'THEIR PRODUCTS ARE NUCLEAR DEATH'.

Or, as this is still England and we're a bit reticent, just keep going into work. Most of your colleagues will assume they were mistaken about you being sacked. If you keep your head down you can go in every day, read the paper, check your email, etc, and if you keep doing it long enough they'll probably start paying you. You might even get promoted.

GETTING A NEW JOB

There are no jobs. Your best bet is to *create* a job, something that's never been done before. Here are some starter tips:

DUELLIST

Offer to fight duels for people, then run away with the money after sending an email to both parties that says YOU WON, I KILLED HIM FOR YOU. They'll be too scared to call the police.

Wanker!

SPONSORED PERSON

Get sponsored. These days people send the money upfront, removing the necessity to do anything. Keep the money. Those kids in Africa would do the same for you.

SPOKESMAN

Become a spokesman. Just open a website on the day of any crisis – water, war, celebrity death – and claim to be the spokesman for the topic. Charge for your opinions, no matter how foolish they are.

FALSE-IDENTITY MAN

Pretend to be someone else. Members of Status Quo, sons of playwrights, film stars, all these people have been victims of organic identity theft as conmen go round getting free meals, hotel rooms and entertainment by claiming to be them. Be imaginative. Tell people you are the real Sting and the one on TV is a ringer, in case pop fans decide to assassinate him. Claim you are the heir to the throne, or would be if King George VI hadn't killed your grandfather in a bare-knuckle boxing contest.

BUSKER

You don't even need a song; most commuters hurry past and only hear the odd bar or two. Simply learn three seconds of 'Blowing In The Wind' and repeat until rich.

CHAPTER 3

TREACHEROUS TRADES

Do you remember when as a youth, sitting in classrooms and learning things that would never be useful to you, like French and Art History, you would see other youths walking past your school, youths who had been lucky enough to leave school before you and who even at a tender teen age had jobs, and money which they could use to buy drinks and fund sex with? Early leavers seemed to have all the fun. These youths might have been working in a domestic arena, they might have spent their lives round other people's houses, present and future, but they were having fun and earning money, something you have always found hard to manage, the fun being had generally when the money wasn't being earned and vice versa. Never mind that these days you have a 'proper' job which almost covers your enormous monthly mortgage, and that nearly every year you can have an expensive holiday in a place you don't want to go but your family do – your previously youthful contemporaries may now be as old as you but they still seem to be living an exciting 'on the edge' lifestyle, cash in hand, can of lager in hand, driving more exciting cars than you have, clearly having no mortgage worries in either their UK or Spanish homes, and also enjoying a freedom in matters of both sex and tattoos that you can only dream of.

So perhaps now is the time to hone your DIY skills to a vaguely professional level . . . but be careful. Those public-information films from the 1970s were right. The Home is a Death Trap!

ELECTRICIAN

So here's a question – how many Dangerous Middle-Aged Men does it take to change a light bulb? One – you! The centrepiece of all home improvement, DIY and so on. Electricity is everything, because it fuels the telly, the DVD, the computer and the microwave – the four horsemen of the modern hearth. Without it, we are stumbling Bronze Age hippies. With it, we can do anything. No wonder, then, that its secrets are so closely guarded and its high priests so highly paid. And in a world where men of a certain age, even though they have lived in the SAME HOUSE for a quarter of a century, do not entirely know where the fuse box is, or indeed what they would do if they found it, the electrician is king. No wonder they charge five hundred quid just to leave their presumably beautifully lit dens.

You may be keen to learn the skills of the electrician, but remember: these are actual skills. You can't just tell the wife, 'Don't worry, darling, I'll soon have the computer and the DVD working.' Can you? Well, yes, thanks to the simple tenet of Dangerous DIY you can. The glory of this philosophy is a simple one: if you do something and it doesn't work, well, it wasn't working before, was it? Just keep sticking wires into sockets and swapping fuses around until something happens. The truth about most gadgets now, you see, is that, because nobody knows how they work, the people who built them have to make them *easy to switch on*. You might have no idea how the furry metal bar at the bottom of your kettle makes the water boil, but you know that the light-up plastic switch on the handle makes the furry bar do whatever it does, and if you can make that work, bob's your uncle.

But do bear in mind that electricity is innately Dangerous. Quite why we ended up deciding to use it to power all our stuff instead of water or steam is a mystery, but use it we do. So think on – whenever you go to work with electricity take precautions. Rubber gloves, rubber boots, rubber trousers . . . in fact, a full frogman outfit is your safest option. Turn everything off before you start, because you never know, there might be some residual electricity lurking in some old sockets. Take the batteries out of everything. Take everything out of everything. In fact, just take it all back to the shop and buy a new one. She'll never know.

CARPENTER

People have been doing carpentry for literally thousands of years, so you'd think it would be embedded in our gene pool by now. After all, kids are born with language skills, so surely knocking off the odd chair now and then should be part of our hereditary skillset. But no: it seems that the only people who can do things with saws and nails are actual trained carpenters. When you think about it like that, it makes complete sense that Jesus was a carpenter; after all, he could turn water into wine and feed the Five Thousand, neither of which are much more difficult than building a shelf.

The problem with carpentry is that everything has to be straight, like Christian rock. But unlike Christian rock, carpentry

'If you could see the things I've seen
When I'm cleaning windows.'

also has to be good, because carpentry tends to involve stuff that people put things on, often themselves. (The history of carpentry is essentially the history of storage, from cupboards to mugs to beds, all of which are inventions into which you place other things.) Thus it is quite hard to fake carpentry. Also you can lose a thumb. Sadly, the only solution to being a carpenter is to learn to do it properly. This means actual skill, and no reward, and also, if we're honest, these days you can buy cupboards and tables and mugs and so on ready made.

We would suggest you really don't bother – but there are one or two situations where carpentry is both useful and Dangerous. Well, there are two. Escaping, and Being A Magician. Escaping, because if you can build a bridge or a dugout canoe, you'll be very popular with the other people trying to escape, and they'll let you do all the post-escape interviews. As for Being A Magician, you need to build your own props otherwise you'll just forget where the Beautiful Assistant is and saw her head off, which will do your love life no good.

Normally we'd advise against bothering, but Escaping and Being A Magician are such exciting and Dangerous things to learn that it's worth it. And even if you do then fail to escape or saw your assistant in three instead of in half, you can at least make your own toast racks.

LABOURER

Farm labouring is spectacularly Dangerous. It's hard to believe, but most farm labourers seem to spend their time virtually throwing themselves under combine harvesters. Then there's people being knocked down by tractors, threshed by threshers, gored by bulls and bullied by flocks of sheep. It's much more Dangerous than joining the SAS.

If you fancy some physical labour but don't actually want to end up on the prongs of a pitchfork, we recommend urban labour. Construction seems to be an idyllic trade in which to work. Most construction workers spend their lives drinking tea high above the city while occasionally shouting down compliments to passers-by.

PLUMBER

The centrepiece of the It that you can't Do Yourself – plumbing is the Holy Grail of Do It Yourself, the mostly closely guarded of all home-maintenance skills. Why? Because we can live without electricity and wooden tables but we cannot live with a toilet that doesn't work or heating that doesn't get hot or things that we can't wash. Water, the element from which we all unwisely crawled, is still essential to us. Nowadays, sometimes we wish that our aquatic ancestors had sat down before they left the oceans and asked: are we REALLY going to be all right without water? Because plumbers charge a fortune and once we've got rid of our gills there is no going back.

But here we are, reliant on water, and how sensible it would be if we all learned to do our own plumbing. Surely, we reason, it can't be that hard: it's mostly replacing the odd ball-cock anyway, isn't it? Not really, it seems: plumbing is a hard discipline akin to Kung Fu and the only way to do it is either to be descended from plumbers or to go to evening classes.

But be warned: plumbing is a genuinely Dangerous job. Apart from the very real faint possibility that you might drown in your basement after failing to fix a leaky washing machine, there's also the fact that plumbers spend a lot of time working with toilets. And that can't be fun.

WINDOW CLEANER

There are two kinds of window cleaner. One is the kind that you are: stepladder, bucket of warm and soapy water, and some old newspapers because you read somewhere that old newspapers are great for cleaning windows, except that when you do it the newspapers go soggy and stick to the glass. This impresses no one even if you've got one of those really quite nice metal squeegees.

The other kind of window cleaner is far more Dangerous to be but also lots more fun. This is the kind of window

Clearly a stag night to remember.

cleaner who lives in a 'cradle' and gets to go up and down very tall enormous glass buildings with, presumably, an absolutely enormous squeegee. Window cleaners of this stripe also get to risk their lives leaning over, and also wobbling about when one of the cables holding up the cradle slips. On the plus side, they sometimes get to do industrial espionage by taking photographs of secret plans through the glass and, if they're really lucky, they often find themselves being knocked out by Bruce Willis in action movies before he smashes the cradle through the glass and shoots some terrorists.

Yes, you should see the things people have seen, when they're cleaning windows.

CLEANER OF GUTTERING

It's definitely quite dangerous, as once you're up that steep risky ladder crows will think you want their eggs and will peck you, while squirrels with no real justification will attack you from all angles. Even if you are unharassed by the animal kingdom (and don't forget wasps' nests under the eaves) then there's always the very real danger of the guttering collapsing and you falling to your death (we're presuming it was you who thought you could safely affix guttering in the first place). All this is quite dramatic really, especially when you consider that this clearly Dangerous activity is one with No Real Job Description. Sinister, no?

Generally life on a roof is dangerous. Thatched roofs tend to burst into flames at the slightest provocation. Tiled roofs were designed for you to slip off. Rain doesn't help. Roofers are apparently considered to be insane by other members of the building trade, which could be caused by all the pigeon crap found on windowsills, which is fatal.

But you can impress your friends by spending all your spare time high up. Sit on a girder that's being winched into the sky. Best of all, pretend to be a Native American, because they don't get vertigo. Be careful, though; you don't want your posthumous nickname to be Falls Like Stone.

CHAPTER 4

A CIRCUS LIFE

For the middle-aged man there comes a time in his life when he seeks romance. Not always the romance of the candlelit dinner, or the romance of life on the high seas, but something even more glamorous – the circus! As a child, perhaps you thought of life in the circus, travelling the world in exotic caravans, the smell of sawdust and lion dung underfoot, late-night card games with midgets, and a little dog in a ruff for company. Perhaps you will marry one of a pair of conjoined twins. Anything is possible in the circus, and, amazingly, in an age of Health and Safety craziness (@ *The Daily Mail*) and Political Correctness Gone Mad (ditto), circuses still thrive. Admittedly, you're no longer allowed to bait bears or fire kittens from cannons but, by and large, anything goes. And circuses are, with all due respect to the many fine institutions we've all heard of, not always entirely safe and ordinary places. In short, if you're tempted by the Dangerous Life, or if you're just waiting for that interview for the French Foreign Legion, hey diddley dee, it's a circus life for ye. As this Dangerous Guide to Circus Romance indicates.

THE TRAPEZE

Clearly Dangerous, especially as your lower man parts are all but out for anyone to see. What with all those narrow metal bars and those terrified partners eager to grab something – anything – as they hurtle through the air, we're not sure that we can recommend this, especially as the only good thing about it is that you might meet women afterwards, and frankly the state of your lower man parts after an hour on the trapeze will be far from magnificent. So try something else. Like:

TIGHTROPE WALKING

One of the weirdest activities known to man, so weird that the people in the world who are the best at it are the French. Which means it must be arty. French people only do things which are arty. And what could be more arty than tightrope walking? Thinking about it, wire walking is sort of related to the trapeze, in that it's got people in ballet clothes with long moustaches doing difficult and clever balancing, but – and it's an important but – it's all rather prosaic. The trapeze is a blur of flying bodies and sequined grace. The tightrope is a man pushing a wheelbarrow with a poodle in it along a rope. That's fairly risky but not very exciting. We find it hard to imagine the *petits enfants* of old Paris lisping, '*Maman*, can we please go to see the man who pushes a poodle in a wheelbarrow on a rope? He has the moustaches complicated'.

But tightrope walking (is it called that because you wear tights and it's on a rope?) is Dangerous, and romantic, even though in a circus your fall is more likely to be broken by lion dung. Talking of which . . .

'Hmm, I think I'm being followed.'

LION-TAMING

As everyone knows, cats are bastards. And none more so than the big cats. Never mind Tiddles trying to claw your eyes out as you doze or bringing in dead birds as a feudal tribute to her hated master, lions and tigers are – basically – a normal cat's idea of what a cat should be. Very big, very Dangerous and very often asleep. But not, which is great for Dangerousness, often enough.

There are many opportunities for Danger and harm with lions outside the circus, but it's hard to get into them. For example, there are quite a few lions in Africa but access to them is expensive (you have to go to Africa) and you stand a good chance of being shot by some do-gooder white South African who's been bored out of his mind ever since the end of apartheid put an end to his occasional manhunts. Similarly, safari parks are a risk for the Danger seeker, unless your idea of a thrill is having your car dismantled by loads of monkeys. Zoos are a no-no since, thanks to hundreds of idiotic young boys whose one ambition is to fall into a bear cage, zoo-keepers are far too alert to any attempts by members of the public to engage with their charges.

So, as with many other things, it's left to circuses to provide us with our only legal sources of Danger. And here is your chance to have Dangerous fun with lions, by becoming a lion-tamer. Can there be a funkier job? You get a uniform, a splendid moustache (moustaches seem to be even more rife amongst the circus community than they are in the gay community, which is saying something). You have a large audience, and people think you are brave, or deranged, or both. And best of all, it bloody well is Dangerous.

The whole act, of course, loses something of its thrill when you learn that the lions are generally more drugged-up than a British indie group, and are no more capable of attacking you than they are of learning Spanish. So why not earn the respect of animal-rights activists and forgo the giant pills in the raw steaks before the show? In fact, why not get rid of the giant steaks altogether? You want your team to be alert on the night and there's nothing more alert than a hungry lion. And surely that whip is barbaric? And the chair – well, that would just wind a lion up, being offered a chair. No, your best bet is to go into that cage full of starving killers with no offensive weapons whatsoever.

Not that you've lost your duty to entertain the crowd. A wide range of amusing lion-friendly props is required. If you've no whip, just run up to Leo and tickle him. He may like it, he may not. It's hard to say. Frankly, everything's a lottery with lions. Remember to clean their teeth with a big toothbrush and put your head right inside their mouths to check for decay. What could possibly go wrong?

ELEPHANT PERSON

Someone's got to do it. And walking behind an elephant, while necessary and hygienic, is very Dangerous. Especially when it's one of those elephants that's been taught to sit down. Not a nice way to go, wedged up Jumbo's bumbo.

BEING A STRONGMAN

A circus strongman is like a body builder only a bit lazy. They never seem to actually work out, and they only really lift one weight – a big pole with two sagging black balls on the end. Sometimes they will pull a coal cart with their teeth. Sometimes they will be a foil for the clowns. To be honest, it doesn't seem much like proper work. But it is fairly Dangerous in that most strongmen seem to be fifty and are quite likely to have a spectacular hernia during their performance. Hop LA!

CLOWNING

Becoming a clown is one of the most mysterious callings in the world. Not because it's a noble, ancient art that has its roots in the *commedia dell'arte*, but because, basically, what kind of idiot git would want to become a clown? The money's awful, the clothes are vile, the hours unsocial and, worst of all, clowns aren't funny. No clown in the history of the world has ever done, said or even thought anything remotely funny. Clowns are absolutely horrible. The favoured uniform for serial killers is a clown suit. Coincidence? No. Only really sick people would actually want to dress as a clown. In a perfect

Hard to believe that we are descended from these primitive creatures.

world, the song 'Tears Of A Clown' would be celebratory, not sad.

So if you become a clown, you are doing, in a way, something quite extraordinarily brave and foolish. You are one of the Few. One of the stupid, annoying, unfunny Few, but one of the Few nevertheless. Perhaps – good Lord, what a thought – by being a clown you are doing something noble. Frankly, it doesn't bear thinking about.

Be a clown! the song says, and if you do that, surely you are in Dangerous territory. First to go will be your home life;

unless your wife is insane and your kids love having Bozo the Dad for a father, your family will leave you the moment they see that red nose on the kitchen table. Next will be your friends; because who wants to go to the pub with Ronald McDonald? And then the last to leave will be your sanity; because it's impossible to believe that anyone could live the life of a clown and not go stark, staring mad.

Oh and the other Danger? Come on - every night you go out in front of an audience of people accustomed to the highs of modern entertainment and the very best in comedy from film and TV. And every night you drive a not-funny car, pour buckets of water down your pants, and hope that a little dog dressed as Sir Francis Drake will make people laugh. That, reader, is Dangerous.

CHAPTER 5

PERILOUS PURSUITS

Why just let Dame Danger be your boss at work when there are any number of alternative pastimes for her to supervise that would give you that unforgettable feeling of 'Isn't it great to be alive . . . but for how long?' . . .

RUSSIAN ROULETTE

The daddy of them all. Played often by Frenchmen who have written some bad poetry and no longer care about life, it was also a favourite of Graham Greene who whiled away many dull hours nearly blowng his brains out. It also features in the movie *The Deer Hunter*, where it seems it was also popular in Vietnam. With such widespread market penetration, surely Russian Roulette is a candidate high up the list for inclusion in the next Olympic Games? Our shooting teams are already amongst the best in the world, and a sport like Russian Roulette would also afford upcoming young athletes the chance to participate as older athletes suffer immediate early retirement.

Even better, given that you don't need any particular skill

to play Russian Roulette, perhaps it should be considered as a replacement for *The X Factor* or *Pop Idol* or any of those shows where talentless people are paraded in front of us for entertainment. You'd really have to be keen to succeed in show business to be a contestant on *Russian Roulette Idol.*

BARE-KNUCKLE BOXING

I t's time this one was brought back. These days, boxing is just too namby-pamby. As other sports go into meltdown with protective clothing in cricket, rugby and even soccer (people are as we speak working on designs for soccer helmets), surely the trend should be reversed, and for once should have a sport stand alone and proud without any protective clothing?

And if it's inhumane for people to hit other people, why not bring in some of the feistier members of the animal kingdom? Kangaroos enjoy a bit of boxing. Imagine the viewing figures you'd get if Mike Tyson returned to the world stage to beat the crap out of a wallaby. And swans – they can break someone's arm with their wing, we're

Not only bare-knuckle but that moustache is sharp as a razor and could have your chin off.

told, although nobody has ever seen this happen. Let's petition the swans' legal owner – Her Majesty The Queen – to allow swans to enter competitive sport. Swans versus kangaroos? It could happen.

SYNCHRONISED SWIMMING

Not innately Dangerous, because its entire wussy history has only taken place in swimming pools, where the worst thing that can happen is somebody might get an old plaster stuck to their leg. The Dangerous Man should get together an Extreme synchronised swimming team and practise off the shark-riddled coast of Australia, or in quicksand.

HAVE-A-GO HERO

The police, who we are told are more concerned with filling out forms concerning health and safety issues than catching the real criminals these days, are constantly advising the general public not to be a 'have-a-go hero'. The problem with this policy is the use of the word 'hero'. No sane person is going to want to be told not to be something cool like a hero. If the police used the phrase 'have-a-go pillock', then you'd see personal bravery and Dangerous behaviour vanish.

In the meantime, before the police realise their error, we suggest that if you want to live Dangerously being a have-a-go hero is a good place to start. It's an active life, running down the street after muggers and jewel thieves. You get rewards from shopkeepers, and you probably meet women who find it attractive to go out with have-a-go heroes. You'll get in the paper, especially if you're an older have-a-go hero.

The only downside is that you might not be very good at it and could end up being quite badly hurt by villains. We suggest therefore that you arrange for some friends to commit small crimes and practise on them before moving on to more dangerous villains.

John Smeaton, the have-a-go hero baggage handler.
If only he spent less time tackling terrorists and more
time handling baggage, our suitcases might not
still be in Cairo.

'Yes, it's definitely a bomb . . .'

AMATEUR BOMB-DISPOSAL

Just listen to police radios and every time there's a report of an unexploded bomb turn up in an unmarked van dressed as a soldier and take over. Most UXBs (technical term) are very old and can be defused by cutting the blue wire. Or is it the red wire? No, it's the blue one. No, red . . .

WEARING THE WRONG COLOURS TO A FOOTBALL MATCH

Self-explanatory, really, but be careful. Football teams change their strips so often these days that you might end up just looking out of date rather than provocative as you sit down among the Celtic fans in your Rangers strip. Instead of starting a fight, the other fans might feel sorry for you and perhaps even organise a collection so you can buy a new strip.

DRUG TAKING

Try a cocktail of drugs. Literally. Get a lot of drugs, grind them up and put them in a pint mug of vodka with crushed ice and a miniature parasol. There's nothing more exciting than random drug abuse. Think of the Dangerous fun you can have just by visiting the medicine cabinet. If it's half as well stocked as your drinks cabinet, you've at least got some paracetamol, valium, Night Nurse, lithium, temazepam, ventolin and Calpol. And that's without even paying a trip to the doctor and claiming you need amphetamine for your diet issues or morphine because your leg has come off.

Taking drugs is very Dangerous, and also slightly random. Some rock stars live their lives on illegal drugs that they've bought from people with no medical qualifications whatsoever. Other rock stars die from ingesting perfectly legal drugs that they've had prescribed for them by actual doctors. You just don't know what's going to happen. You can live for years like William Burroughs, sane and happy on a daily diet of heroin, or you can have a horrific time like Brian Wilson, off his rocker sitting in a sandpit because of all the LSD he took.

And then there are the side effects. Many drugs are illegal and you can go to jail, where you can get even more drugs and they can't arrest you for it. Most drugs are addictive, which is more annoying than anything else because just when you're about to sit down and watch *QI* you suddenly have a terrible craving to take lots of drugs, and there goes your evening.

The most extraordinary side effect of drugs that we've ever heard of comes, aptly enough, from Thomas De Quincy's excellent book *Confessions of an English Opium-Eater*. Elsewhere De Quincy recounts the story of Samuel Taylor Coleridge, whose own opium use became so extreme that, to try and break himself of the habit, Coleridge hired a man whom he instructed to prevent him from entering pharmacies and buying more opium. Unfortunately for the man, when Coleridge was prevented from going into the pharmacy he had a tendency to attack the man he'd hired. (The man did later get his revenge, we believe, by going round to Coleridge's house and pretending to be from Porlock, thus making Coleridge forget a whole poem he'd just written.)

DRUG TESTING

Lots of fun. Not only do you get paid but you also get to be the first to take drugs that nobody else has ever had before and whose properties are unknown, so you're like a test pilot but of the internal world. Man. Also the side effects could be at worst lethal and at best exciting, like in *Willy Wonka*. Besides, it's more interesting than just getting drunk, isn't it?

CHEESE ROLLING

This is extremely dangerous, because you're essentially doing low running. The cheese rolls down the hill quite happily. You, however, don't. It is a highly skilled occupation whose main downside is not only that you can really hurt yourself, but also everyone will laugh at you when they hear *how* you hurt yourself.

CARRYING FLAMING BARRELS OF PITCH THROUGH THE STREETS OF OTTERY SAINT MARY

This is one of the least safe things you can do in Devon. Every year festival-goers and revellers do just that – run down the road with a burning barrel on their shoulders. It is highly Dangerous but has to be a lot of fun. Although we're not sure how you would get the opportunity to practise.

'Ha ha! This is fun! Ow! OW!'

RUNNING WITH THE BULLS

Again, the Dangers are obvious, especially if you become confused, get turned around and run at the bulls instead of away from them. Remember, the bulls are not naturally

'My goodness! Is that a – bull?
RUN! RUN FOR YOUR LIVES!'

inclined to attack people, just confused and possibly dis-
tressed at the effeminate attire of the runners in their red
berets and neckerchiefs.

BEING A VOLUNTEER AT A MAGIC OR HYPNOTISM SHOW

Fancy a bit of attention? Want some Danger in public? Then volunteering to assist a magician or a hypnotist is always good. Volunteering to help a hypnotist can have side effects – in a way, you're a bit like a beagle being put on sixty Rothmans a day – but you might learn a new skill. Like running naked through Dorchester, or bursting into mad laughter whenever someone mentions chickens. Magicians are more fun, as you are not under their hypnotic mental control. For example, when you're first invited onstage and the magician says, 'Now, we've never met before, have we?' agree with him and then turn to the audience and say, 'That's what he told me to say. Actually, we were at school together,' and run like hell. Remember, he has knives AND trained doves.

CHAPTER 6

ABSURD
OCCUPATIONS

One of the risks – the real risks, that you can't avoid if you're a middle-aged man – is the creeping sense of absurdity that threatens to come up behind you and throw a sack over your head. As children, we are told, we act like children and so forth, but later we put away childish things – well, clearly Saint Paul, who tucked that little gem into one of his many letters to the increasingly vexed Corinthians ('Any post? Oh no, not again') had never been on eBay – and become old and presumably learn wise things and later people will come to us and marvel at how much we know and how few teeth we have.

In reality, as children we just basically run around taking stuff for granted – Dogs can be made to bark! Noise is exciting! Dad is angry! – and then we pass into a terrible cynicism known as adolescence. Many of us never recover from this, partly because in life there is lots to be cynical about. But many of us, as time passes, and life's little ironies, move into a second more dangerous stage, never recover from this. Reading the papers and watching television, one becomes not jaded and cynical but overwhelmed with a sense of the ridiculous. You don't get angry because some gimp in the public sector who is supposed to be looking after our interests has given himself a fifty billion quid bonus. You just accept the absurdity of it, albeit in a slightly twitchy, straitjackety way. You don't smash all the windows when you hear that a celebrity with no talent has died and been lauded in terms that would make Caligula blush. You just sit there and let the whole nonsensicalness wash over you.

This sense of life's absurdity is not healthy. It can lead to a certain giggly, hysterical recklessness. In a younger person or a wise old hermit this sort of thing needs to be kept on a short leash. But in a middle-aged man who's already getting a bit Dangerous, a sense of the absurd can be easily converted into a sense of the Dangerously Absurd. This is, we suspect, why you often see grown men engaging in the kind of activity that only 1950s students or people afflicted by Jazz Age crazes used to undertake. The kind of things that fools used to do to get into the *Guinness Book of Records* but these days they do without even calling up Ross McWhirter. Things like crossing the Atlantic in a bathtub. Or carrying an Aga kitchen range across France. Or being the head of ITV. Absurd, pointless, rewardless activities that only have a point if you believe life to be essentially ridiculous, or you've got a book deal.

Here now, if you favour a common-senseless approach to being a Dangerous Middle-Aged Man, is our guide to being Dangerously Absurd. The usual health and safety warnings apply, with an extra one – if you do any of these things, not only are you in Danger of hurting yourself but also, even if you survive, chances are everyone will take you for a complete tool. So think on, unless it's too late for that sort of thing. In which case, welcome to *The Dangerous Book for Middle-Aged Men*'s Top Five Dangerously Absurd Activities.

NATURIST BEE-KEEPING

What better way can there be of living the utterly organic lifestyle? Bees, when they're not busy going extinct or hiding in Peru, not only knock out loads of honey, hardly any of which they seem to touch themselves, but also do not give a stuff about what you are wearing. Similarly, nudism – like bee-keeping – is something few of us try until it's too late. When we had the kind of bodies that people might conceivably climb up cliffs to look at through binoculars, we were most of us too shy to expose ourselves. Nowadays, like most nudists, we have the sort of physique that most resembles chucking-out time at a plasticine factory, or a terrible accident in a waxworks.

No wonder we're running out of bees!

But bees don't care about that. They'll sting you whether you're head to toe in Ozwald Boateng or you're walking round with your knackers out for all to see. Talking of which, if you actually do succeed in making some honey, don't be surprised if nobody wants to eat it. The thought of mid-lifey privates hovering anywhere near a jar of tasty honey is rarely an appealing one. Even Winnie the Pooh might think twice if he knew Eeyore had been having a dangle near the hive.

RIVERDANCE IN A REAL RIVER

You think aquacising is hard? Water aerobics? At least with those two pool-bound activities you get to wave your arms up and down above the surface of the water. No such luck with this one. Irish dancing requires, for no reason known to anyone, that you keep your arms by your sides throughout while making weird sort of 'Pinocchio needs the loo' movements with your legs. And if that seems pointless on land, imagine how much more ridiculous it'll be waist deep in water.

Why not start small – maybe doing a bit of Lord of the Dance-style action in your local pool before stepping up to a small stream and eventually really going for it by giving it Riverdance in, say, the Manchester Ship Canal or the Thames. What about trying it in Paris? You'd gives a whole new meaning to the phrase 'in Seine'.

AVANT GARDE OPERA KARAOKE

To ensure a high risk factor, go to karaoke contests with your own karaoke tapes and, when your name comes up, give them a rendition of your favourite difficult opera moments. Never mind 'Nessun Dorma', how about a couple of selections from Alban Berg's atonally bleak *Lulu*? They'll be baying for your blood as you wanly croak your way across a scale most musicians don't recognise, let alone members of the public looking for a nice bit of slightly tuneless Abba on a Friday night. Might not sound that Dangerous? Trust us, there are pubs in East London, Burnley and the Fens where a reasonably good version of 'Mamma Mia' will guarantee you a bludgeoning, let alone the final aria from *Nixon In China*. Give it a go!

COMPETITIVE BUSKING

Busking is one of the most horrific activities known to man, so you should feel no shame in ruining a busker's day. Simply stake out your busker and as soon as he starts doing 'Blowing In The Wind', whip out a guitar and *join in*. In fact, plug in an electric guitar, or set up a drum kit. Not only will the busker try and kill you but members of the public may encourage him, because how often do you see a fight to the death between buskers?

LIVE 'SPOILERS'

We all hate it when we accidentally read in the paper or online how our favourite TV series ends, or what happens at the climax of a movie we've waited ages to see. So enjoy yourself at the expense of film- and theatregoers by sitting through whatever piece of rubbish is huge right now and, about thirty minutes in, when they're all getting into it, say, 'It's terrible how she dies' or 'The inspector did it.' There is no greater feeling of power, and certainly nothing like that feeling allied to the sense of terror as you flee the cinema or theatre. Live life on the edge!

CHAPTER 7

DERRING-DO

Imagine if all archaeologists were like this. Wouldn't
Time Team *be about a million times better?*

There is a thin line, as everybody knows, between bravery and stupidity. Therefore if it's easy for stupid people to perform extraordinary acts of valour and, presumably, get their heads blown off, it should be fairly easy for smart people like yourself to carry out acts of minor bravery and get lots of medals, press coverage and sex. Not that we want to be cynical about gallantry and the like, just that surely there are short cuts to the top in this as in every field.

So rehearse that stiff-upper-lip response to all enquiries, remind your batman to get in extra supplies of Silvo for medal polishing, invest in a bulletproof PR, and sit back as you enjoy this short guide to the best, and most rewarding, forms of Dangerous Derring-Do.

WHISTLEBLOWING

This is a very Dangerous thing to do, because it can be viewed as illegal or even treasonous, it has enormous effects on public figures and institutions, and, most importantly of all, it draws attention to you. You can't just go to the media and say, 'Here are some top-secret papers, everyone is corrupt, and, by the way, if anyone asks, it wasn't me who told you.' YOUR NAME WILL COME OUT. And your bosses will be angry, and the law will be brought into force against you, and you may even go to jail. It's by no means safe, and the only slight consolation you may obtain is that of fickle, empty fame, leading to fickle, empty success with your autobiography, fickle, empty appearances on chat shows, fickle, empty wealth and lots of fickle, empty sex. So think on.

SPYING

Spying. The quickest way to be a spy is this. Just go to MI5 and tell them you're a Russian spy. They can't check! Then offer to become a double agent. Then nip round the Russian embassy and tell them you're with MI5. Then try the American embassy. Most embassies are quite close together, so frankly you could do the lot in an afternoon.

And, just to go into the topic a little more thoroughly, here are some more detailed spying tips:

1. Choose the country you spy on wisely. Some countries don't really mind – Belgium, for example, might well be delighted that you think they're worth spying on and would probably help you out, giving you free samples of their weapons programme and so forth – but others, like America, say, and China – would take it pretty badly and might even shoot you. You could try asking them for money to not spy on them, but they might shoot you anyhow. The trick is to find a country that would be annoyed by you spying on them but not so annoyed that they'd shoot you. Italy, perhaps; they might enjoy it, and even if they don't, they may well send beautiful Italian lady spies out to seduce you. This would probably be all right.

2. Before you start being a spy, write down who you are on a piece of paper and put it somewhere safe. Most spies now seem to have their identities erased as soon as they leave the house. Of course, you will have lost your memory so you won't know where you've written down your old identity, so the best thing to do is commit a small offence – traffic, noise pollution – and six months later your local council or penalty-fine enforcement agency will come after you. And

they're a lot more relentless and dangerous than the CIA. If nothing else it would have saved Matt Damon a whole lot of bother in the *Bourne Identity* series.

3. Avoid normal spying, which has become very dull. Even if you do remember your own identity or are not shot, you will spend most of your time in a very dull office block on the Thames looking at pictures of sullen young men. The high point of the day will be going to Tesco Metro to get your lunch, during which time you will mistakenly put an unidentified item in the bagging area and the scanner thing will accidentally erase your identity. So what's the alternative?

4. The alternative is industrial espionage. It's great because, essentially, all you do is sneak into design laboratories and nick new stuff. Anything, if the ads are to be believed, from iPods to Porsches. What better job could there be for the Dangerous Middle-Aged Man than stealing gadgets and cool cars? Imagine: one minute you're waiting for the bus in the rain and the next someone calls up and asks if you fancy stealing a Stealth bomber and some brand new digital camcorders. Brilliant!

5. And then there's the lazy option – being a 'sleeper' agent. Sadly not quite as idle as you might hope, sleeper agents are those people who deliberately take on a different identity, as opposed to having their brains wiped, and live dull lives as estate agents in Hampshire until one day a coded message comes in and they have to kill Jack Straw. At least, that's what they tell the police afterwards.

HOSTAGE NEGOTIATING

We're not clear on how you become a hostage negotiator. Do you start by persuading cats to come down from trees? Were you very good at convincing ex-girlfriends not to put your CD collection in a skip? Or did you just live next door to some kidnappers and thought you could save everyone time and bother by getting them to release the neighbours? Whatever the truth of it, being a hostage negiotator is a tricky job because, unlike the civil service or the entertainment industry, you are judged entirely by results. Civil servants can coast for years because nobody will ever find out how idle they are. Music-business executives know that if they never sign a band they can't be sacked. But hostage negotiators – well, they kind of have to save all the hostages, really, otherwise they're more like hostage let-be-shot-ers. So being a hostage negotiator really does mean you have to get down and get with it. It's tough; but there are ways round it. Offer them unexpected deals, like holidays, or supermarket vouchers. Establish a rapport: pretend to like the same music, or to know their cousin. Pretend to BE their cousin – 'This *is* Marcel, you idiot!' Or just tell them that the hallway is full of giant radio-controlled bears with metal teeth. That often works in these situations.

But be warned – the job of hostage negotiator carries with it the very real danger that you might make a complete arse of yourself. Look, if you can bear to, at the failed hostage negotiations of the otherwise loveable Terry Waite, envoy to the Church of England, who not only made a pig's ear of getting John McCarthy and Brian Keenan released, but also – being a sort of vicar and therefore a paid fun-damper – ruined the one pleasure they had, namely telling rude stories, by getting chained to the same radiator as them. If you are

46

still not put off, well done. But bear in mind that ignominy is itself a form of Danger, and nothing is more ignominious than this fact: that the phrase 'Terry Waite's garden' is used about someone who has a lot of pubic hair. If you don't mind people speculating on the state of your nethers after, like Terry, they've spent 1,736 days without being attended to, then hostage negotiator is the job for you!

FOREIGN LEGION

The French Foreign Legion are, as they say, rock. Rock hard. Like the SAS, only not as cuddly. Unshaven, wearing those absurd hats, and living in big white forts, the French Foreign Legion are in some ways the opposite of *Hello!* magazine – they don't care who you are – and in others the same – they like to kill people. But they never bloody take a day off. Even the Marines have holidays, even the Parachute Regiment have the odd day off, and even the SAS get to visit their mums. But the French Foreign Legion never let up. It's horrible.

So why not try some of the other Foreign Legions? The Danish Foreign Legion would be ideal: milder weather, lots of beer and high-class porn. Or, given

'Nigel! Get down from there!'

47

the small size of our holdings nowadays, a British Foreign Legion would be nice. Most people would have joined in the mistaken belief that it was (all together now) the British Legion. Not militarily very effective, but you do get a cheap pint.

RUSHING A NEST OF MACHINE-GUNS

This is not only one of the most Dangerous things anyone can do but is one of the main ways of winning the Victoria Cross. Frankly, it's become a bit of a cliché. Not to knock any of the very brave men who've done this, but for your purposes, you might run the risk of being thought a bit old-hat if you rush a nest of machine guns. For a start, your actual machine-gunners in said nest might just start looking at each other and saying things like, 'Is this guy for real?' and be so bummed out that yet again someone is rushing their machine-gun nest that they might just let you run in and, instead of shooting at you, just let you stand there like an idiot. Meanwhile all your friends will be saying, 'Hey! What's going on over there? Are you rushing a nest of machine guns? Because we were specifically told not to do that,' and the machine-guys will be calling over 'Can you come and get him?' and it'll all end in tears.

You know, you really don't want to make a fool of yourself.

PLAYING FOOTBALL IN NO MAN'S LAND

This is one of the best Dangerous things that anyone can do. For a start, it's good for you. Football is a very healthy form of exercise; it's both aerobic and builds up muscles, particularly in the legs. Also it's social; you make friends who are both fun to be with and later you could be useful to each other, career-wise. Best of all, for the purposes of being a Dangerous Middle-Aged Man, it looks really Dangerous but it is in fact perfectly safe (so safe that noted vegetarian pacifist Paul McCartney did it in a video). You can run around all day in no man's land, completely comfortable in the fact that nobody is going to shoot you. They can't; they're all playing football.

Of course, there are a few traditional criteria to be observed here. It has to be a war and it really helps to have trenches (they did try it in World War Two, you know, with less success, because they were told to stop it – again, trenches rather than battlefields help with the layout here). And it positively must be Christmas Day. This is essential. There is, after all, no such thing as 'Easter spirit'. But it also limits things again; if your opponents are bloodthirsty followers of Shinto, say, they may not care about Christmas and instead of joining in a general kickabout will probably just lob a grenade at you.

So within these general parameters, feel free to have fun! But if the game is going on too long with no score, you'd be well advised to abandon it rather than suggest a penalty shoot-out.

LEAVING SOME CHOCOLATES IN A LADY'S VILLA

Not, as the name suggests, a bizarre sexual practice favoured by our European cousins but a perfectly reasonable – and Dangerous – romantic activity with which there is nothing wrong. Invented by some ad executive who had to shift a load of boxes of chocolates onto the general public after he saw a James Bond fim (and presumably punched the air and shouted 'Eureka! I've found a way to make men buy boxes of chocolates'), the idea combines both adventure and girliness in uniquely effective doses.

It does have its flaws, true, but as a way of both impressing a lady while looking cool and being a bit Dangerous, there can be nothing better for you as a would-be Dangerous Middle-Aged Man. You get to look good, you don't have to boast to anyone (she'll do that for you) and, unusually for one of the activities in this otherwise risk-is-its-own-rewardy book, you might have sex at the end of it as well.

But plan things properly. First, ensure that the object of your attention is in some sort of island villa or remote mountain hideaway. Even Tesco Direct can put a box of chocolates through the letter box of a flat in Arundel; you have to go the extra mile. Secondly, make sure you have all the things you need for the job. Not just the commando-type bits – ropes and ladders and a helicopter and a scuba thing – but also the stuff that will Get You Noticed by the lady as, for one brief second, your eyes meet before you dive into the briny surf or fly away into the night. For example, it's no good going to all this trouble if you've brought her a bag of wine gums. Presentation is everything here. Also, get a shave and a haircut, wear a really good black pullover – not some skanky V-neck from the market – and practise things like insouciantly blowing kisses. Most importantly, practise blowing kisses from a rope ladder suspended from a hovering helicopter. All your hard work will be in vain if you've not thought things through and you end up trying to fire air kisses at her as you spin round and round at the bottom of a ladder, legs flailing in the rain.

Oh, by the way, times – and ladies – have changed since the original advert aired. If you think that after and despite all that effort on your part, she's going to be impressed by a box of Milk Tray, you're in the wrong job, mate. Milk Tray is what a nine-year-old boy with no pocket money and no idea gets for his granny – and even she chucks it in the bin when he's not looking. What you need to do is visit an actual chocolatier – yes, you're going to Belgium – and have him hand-select an expensive variety of the best chocolates ever made. You'll be broke afterwards but she'll thank you for it.

Finally, and most importantly of all, make a few inquiries before you embark on your task. It renders the whole thing utterly futile if you go to all this trouble only to have a red-faced man in a T-shirt pick up the chocolates and shout, 'Alison! Where did THESE come from?!'

PARACHUTING INTO ENEMY TERRITORY

Tricky, this. It can go well, especially if you're dressed as a nun (default setting for the Germans in World War Two). You land, you're approached by yokels with pitchforks – relax, yokels, you say, I'm a nun, I was just doing some prayers when someone chucks a bag over my head and before you know it, here I am. All right, sister, the yokels say, off you go. Thanks, you say, by the way, does anyone know the way to Bletchley Park? Easy.

But if you've not dressed as a nun it can all go wrong.

Yokels these days are much more suspicious and will think that you're either a terrorist or a paedophile trying a new approach. There is only one way out of this: point at an imaginary television camera in a haystack and tell them they're in a hilarious TV prank show. They'll laugh and laugh.

ORGANISE A MILITARY COUP IN A SMALL BUT OIL-RICH AFRICAN STATE

Is it Dangerous? What do you think? Don't believe us? Well, here's proof. Look at the example of Simon Mann. He had it all going for him when he decided to stage a coup in Equatorial Guinea: funding from lots of rich people, including the idiot-boy son of Margaret Thatcher, a rich country to take over with a population of 500,000 living in abject poverty while its dictator – himself risen to power in a coup –

*'OK, next year we go to Eastbourne
for the summer holidays.'*

siphoned off most of the country's oil revenue himself. Frankly, Simon Cowell could have walked into Equatorial Guinea and proclaimed himself liberator and people would have flocked to his side. But instead Simon Mann cocked it all up so badly that he lost all support and all hope and ended up in a very nasty jail. The moral of our story is this – if you are contemplating a military coup to overthrow the corrupt regime of a small but oil-rich African state, avoid working with Old Etonians.

Actually, that applies to most things.

ESCAPING FROM A PRISON CAMP

Not what it used to be. They used to be such jolly places, full of men from all nations, whittling and forging and building and playing tricks on the guards. In those days you could even build a life-sized glider in the attic, a fact which speaks volumes about those simple times. A glider? Who was in charge of security? A puppy dog? Nowadays prison camps are really, really Dangerous places and you have no chance of escaping. NB: it also doesn't help, despite what you may have heard from certain of the more primitive political parties, to put your name on a National Health waiting list and get released for urgent cosmetic surgery. That doesn't really happen. Our advice is to try and stay out of prison camps, unless your convictions and your incompetence are of equal strength. Just don't do it!

RUNNING BLOODY MILES WITH A MESSAGE

Hugely popular with the Ancient Greeks, one of whom did it after the Battle of Marathon, this is one of those slightly bizarre things that have Derring-Do written all over them but if we're honest will not benefit you in the slightest. Yes, you'll go down in history as the bravest athlete of all, who sacrificed if not his life then at least his knees to bring the good news to his commanding officer, but these days a text should do the trick. And think on this: do you want posterity's tribute to your mighty endeavour to be a lot of bozos dressing up as giant teddy bears for a charity run? No. You don't. The whole thing is fraught with appalling danger. Our Dangerous Classicist (we have one) tells us that the original messenger, one Pheidippides, was so exhausted by his feat that he actually collapsed and died after delivering his message. Yet in spite of this incredible feat, the International Olympic Committee decided to name their very-long-distance running event not after Pheidippides, who had done the actual running, but Marathon, the place he had in fact just run from. Which, when you think about it, is a bit like paying tribute to Douglas Bader by renaming him Colditz.

SUICIDE MISSIONS

How Dangerous is that? You're just not coming back. But think on: nobody will know it was you. We suggest, perhaps cynically, that if your government, religion or employer nominate you to perform some act where you're going to die and your body will never be recovered, get someone else to do it. The world is full of people who, unlike you, really do want to end it all yet are surrounded by do-gooders who want to keep them alive. Why insult these good people with your involuntary and probably botched attempts at suicide when they're champing at the bit to end it all? They'll thank you as you strap them into a kamikaze plane or lower them into a nuclear furnace to turn off a fusion bomb. And best of all, everyone will think it's you and you'll get a medal and, later, you can pose as your own twin brother and collect the life insurance you thoughtfully took out earlier on.

OK, there's nothing more Dangerous than actually topping yourself, and if you've bought this book just to spice up your life a bit you might not relish slipping off this mortal coil just for fun. So why not fake your own death? This central plank of the Reggie Perrin TV series has its roots in reality, both with the 1970s MP John Stonehouse and another John, John Darwin, who at the age of 51 faked his own death in a canoeing accident. Mind you, that went wrong for both of them, and Stonehouse and Darwin both ended up in jail. Darwin's wife also got banged up, whilst his own children officially hate him. Stonehouse was even less lucky, only getting early release from jail after he suffered three heart attacks.

Thinking about it, it's probably easier to actually top yourself.

CHAPTER 8

EVERYDAY DARES

Daring people to do things has an honourable tradition. We can assume that many of the great expeditions and discoveries of the Victorian era were the results of bets in the various gentlemen's clubs of St James's, possibly after everyone had had a bit too much to drink. There is after all not much difference between one ten-year-old saying to another ten-year-old, 'I bet you can't throw a stone over that roof without smashing a window', and one Victorian man with mutton-chop whiskers saying to another Victorian man in a stovepipe hat, 'I'll wager you cannot circumnavigate the globe in a hot-air balloon'. They are essentially the same thing, except that the man who circumnavigates the globe in a hot-air balloon is unlikely to get six months with a tag round his ankle if he fails.

And while we shall be looking at epic dares, it should be said that not all dares need to be on this grand scale. There are many simpler, localised dares that you can attempt. The only limit is your imagination. There are also the new traditions of daring introduced by television shows like *Jackass* and *Punk'd*. All these things add up to one obviously Dangerous fact – if you are a Dangerous Middle-Aged Man, dares are the way to go.

Britain launches its first moon mission.

But before you run out into the street, ready to make a crank call while skateboarding naked around the world for a wager, just take stock for a moment. Because dares offer the most bitter-sweet Dangerous challenge there is: that of looking a bit of a pillock. So read on, and beware!

ZOO INVASION

Scaling the fence at your local zoo has long provided excitement for anyone attempting it, and an interesting anecdote for shocked witnesses. The most popular enclosures to scale are those of lions, pandas and polar bears. But why not buck the trend and go for more unusual animals, like snakes, piranha fish or wasps? You could even do a bit of a practice by breaking into the petting zoo (although don't forget to wash your hands afterwards) which isn't that hard as it's open to the public, and then work your way up to breaking into whatever it is they keep the ants in, and then try the lemurs who have scary eyes but are probably harmless.

Oh, and remember: if you really want to attract attention to yourself, find out when feeding time is and stage your invasion just before that. Nobody wants to jump into an enclosure full of lions only to find they're too full to come over and say hello.

PUNK'D-TYPE STUFF

Punk'd is the direct heir of all those Jeremy Beadle and Dom Joly prank shows, in that it's not funny. The idea is to perform an elaborate prank on somebody – destroying their house, having them jailed, having them murdered – and then hoping that the sheer excitement of realising that they're on television – OH MY GOD! – will cause your victim to forgive you and sign the release forms. We don't recommend these shows, as they're so overdone and old now that your victim will probably, as happened to an acquaintance of ours who pranked an actual violent criminal, get stabbed in the leg.

Far better, and far more fun in a Dangerous way, is to secretly arrange (get a mole at the production company) to be chosen as a 'victim' of some annoying TV prankster and turn the tables on them by, say, pretending you've had a heart attack, or just taking them to court and suing them.

'You're nicked, Jesus.'

STREAKING

A 1970s classic, but one which, like most things from the 1970s, is enjoying something of a revival these days. You don't want to be left out of anything retro, do you now? So why not try streaking at a major sporting event? It's true that lady streakers are usually guaranteed a better reception, but there's still an honourable tradition of streaking amongst men. Plus it gives the police something useful to do with their helmets while concealing yours. Also, it's more genuinely Dangerous these days because of all the security. Back in the day, you could run about with your bits a-whirl and nobody would have said a thing, but nowadays you leap over the barrier and before you know it you're spending the rest of your life in Camp X-Ray with a bag over your head. Well, you did want the attention.

The slightly over-prepared traveller . . .

JACKASS TYPE STUFF

Whenever you see 'Don't try this at home', try it at home. Just as 'Who Dares Wins' is the motto of the SAS, so 'Don't Try This At Home' was surely the motto of the team from *Jackass* TV. Taser yourself, ride down the stairs in a shopping trolley, attach your skateboard to the back of a car – it's all just there for the doing. The essence of *Jackass* and *Dirty Sanchez* and all the other rip-offs is not to do something prankish but to really, really hurt yourself. The other essence of it, by the way, is to make money from hurting yourself and to not die, so if you do find yourself being rolled down the side of Mount Everest in a burning Portaloo, try and sneak a look at your contract before you actually burst into flames.

PHONE PRANKS

The only Danger, frankly, at our time of life, of phoning up, say, Ed Balls and making some weak pun about testicles is that the recipient of your call will just say, 'Good God, how old are you?', trace the call and have you jailed. Not ideal.

CHAPTER 9

EPIC DARES

People in old books do love them. Around the world in 80 days? Why not? Firing yourself from a cannon to the Moon? Easy! Tracking down the rare Giant Rat of Sumatra? Consider it done! They were simpler times, and being Dangerous was a lot easier because everything in those days was pretty dangerous. Nowadays, of course, the world is a lot safer and epic dares are less effective. Around the world in 80 days is ridiculously slow when a jet plane can do it in a few hours. Flying to the Moon is probably the next thing that Virgin Airlines have planned. And the Giant Rat of Sumatra is almost certainly extinct.

So it's clearly time to upgrade our epic dares and make them spanking new and up to date for the modern age. Here's a few to get you going:

VOYAGE TO THE BOTTOM OF THE SEA

Man has walked on the surface of the Moon, climbed the highest mountains and been to both the Poles. Yet we have hardly begun to explore the oceans. This is because they are incredibly deep and if we went down there we would implode from the pressure. So right there you've got a Dangerous activity all to yourself. Even the Cousteaus confined themselves to the odd pootle-about in a bathysphere. Why not get someone to dare you to catch a brace of humpback angler fish? These terrifying-looking fish have huge mouths with lots of teeth and a sort of aerial on their heads and are capable of eating other fish twice their size. And they live two thousand metres below the ocean's surface, so a fishing rod just won't cut it. You'll need a specially reinforced diving bell and a very strong net.

Why not go right to the bottom of the ocean? It's never been done but we bet that people aren't exactly queueing up to go down there, in the supremely pressured dark and wet. You could be the first! And, afterwards, it would be fun because you'd be famous. Afterwards.

POGO-STICKING AROUND THE WORLD

It sounds silly, like travelling around Ireland with a fridge, but think on. For a start, it would be excellent for your health, as you'd be bound to lose weight. It would also have a personal-safety aspect, as snipers would find it hard to bring down a pogoing target, and wild animals would just run away. Nevertheless, there would still be a large element of danger, not least because trying to cross a desert on a pogo stick is incredibly difficult. Very few desert pogo stick expeditions have made the trip successfully. However, you could get people to sponsor you, and raise money for some charity that doesn't mind being associated with this nonsense. And while you're at it, make a point in your pre-pogo-sticking-around-the-world publicity that it's not for Comic Relief because you don't see why they and Children In Need should have a monopoly on all mortally embarrassing fund-raising activities.

CLIMBING MOUNT EVEREST WITHOUT CLIMBING EQUIPMENT

Life is too restricted and we feel hemmed in on all sides. Mountaineers must feel the same way as they trudge up Everest wrapped in restrictive furs and layers of snowproof clothing, wearing thick gloves, weighed down with breathing apparatus and camping equipment, and just longing for the moment when they can throw away their masks and balaclavas. They don't even need all that equipment. If the Yeti can do it, and Sherpas can almost do it, then surely you can, leaping from ledge to ledge like a mountain goat and enjoying your freedom! And when you get to the top, why not pretend you're Finnish and run around naked in the snow, yelling at the top of your voice? Dangerous fun at its best.

'Clothes! That's what I forgot to pack!'

64

PEARL DIVING

Pearl diving is less popular than it was, but it is still practised in America, mostly on the rather excitingly named Lesbo River. In the Persian Gulf it is so engrained in local culture that it has its own music, *fijiri*, which is sung to the pearl-divers to encourage them and tell them they're really good at finding pearls. And it's also one of the few properly risky jobs left in the world. Venezuelan pearl diving was particularly dangerous because the divers used to share the sea with sharks.

Get someone to dare you to dive for your own pearls, which you then are supposed to give to a beautiful woman. Although we would imagine that if you had been diving for pearls at dangerous depths using no breathing apparatus with a load of sharks nosing around, you'd probably want to keep the buggers for yourself.

FINDING THE HOLY GRAIL

This is a tough one. Indiana Jones found it in the film. Dan Brown and lots of other people believe it's a mistranslation of Sang Real which means Holy Blood, and so the Holy Grail is a Frenchwoman or something. Other people think it's behind a wall in a church in Istanbul. Still others just think it's completely made up. But assuming it exists, it would be very hard to find, and you'd probably be hunted down by the Freemasons, the Knights Templar and the lawyers for *The Da Vinci Code*. However, our favourite theory is that the Holy Grail is an actual cup, and it was buried in Somerset by Joseph of Arimathea. There you go, you can have that one for free.

GETTING SOMETHING NAMED AFTER YOU

Many people prefer to be active, however, and will trample through the inhospitable Australian bush just to find a rare species of poisonous tick they can call after themselves. This is OK, but hard to do as most animals have either been discovered or are extinct. Instead of going to such exertions, you may find an easier method of locating your unknown bug is to dramatically lower your own standards of personal hygiene and wait for the unknown bugs to come to you. Much more original and Dangerous is the notion that you contract a disease so rare and horrible that they name it after you. Think of the pride as you are wheeled out at the School of Horrible Diseases and announced to the impressed students in the lecture theatre as 'Mister Alan Frobisher – the first person to contract Alan Frobisher's Disease.' Baby, you're a star!

CHAPTER 10

DANGEROUS ROLE MODELS

Others, lest we forget, have been here before us. History is full of Dangerous Middle-Aged Men. Livingstone, hacking his way through Africa and naming everything after Queen Victoria. Stanley, the journalist who found Livingstone by taking doorstepping to new levels. Malcolm and Donald Campbell, trying to go too fast on land and water. Scott of the Antarctic, the first 42-year-old to not get to the South Pole before the Norwegians. The list is endless. Everything that can be done by a middle-aged man has been done.

But don't worry. As TV talent shows prove, just because something has been done once doesn't prevent it from being done again. In fact, in many ways that's better, because those who went before have, if not exactly ironed out the snags, then showed you what not to do when the time comes to emulate them. So, for example, instead of doing a Captain Oates and saying, 'I am going outside. I may be some time,' and dying for the good of the others, your modern Dangerous man will probably just say, 'I've got a real craving for some dry-roasted peanuts – anyone fancy popping out to the shop for me?'

As a Dangerous Middle-Aged Man, you will want to do what your heroes have done but, unless you are exceptionally

67

jaded (and we have sections in this book which cater for you), you may not want to actually top yourself in the process. So here now is an as it were cigarette-card-style catalogue of Dangerous Heroes for you to learn from.

JAMES BOND

All right, he's not strictly real – although so many people have played him now that they'll probably get round to asking you soon. But James Bond is the ideal Dangerous Man. For a start, he's always in danger. This is good, because it's exciting. And the sort of danger he gets into is not that dangerous, really. For a start, the villain always tries to help him out by not only explaining his plan but telling James Bond how he will die. This is enormously useful as a) it gives James Bond time to think and b) the villain is clearly giving Bond lots of clues on how to escape. 'Now you are suspended over this tank of PIRANHAS (i.e. push the guard in!) by this NYLON ROPE (hint: use that knife you've hidden), and soon I will launch my DEATH RAY at New York (I'll be upstairs – you might want to kill that scientist and steal his radiation suit).'

Emulating Bond also means lots of sex, although you will need a stock of weak one-liners. Again, there are clues. If your sexy lady is wearing snakeskin, when she asks if she should go

The best Doctor Who.

68

you can murmur, 'Serpently not.' If she's a sports-loving lesbian, say, 'Care to play for the other team?' And if she pulls a gun on you, say, 'Can't we have sex instead?' That sort of thing.

But there are real dangers these days for pretend Bonds. For a start, actual spying is grim and chances are a Russian will just come up and poison you without explaining themselves first. That's just not fair.

SIR DAVID AND LORD DICKIE ATTENBOROUGH

Like the ancient giants Gog and Magog, the Attenboroughs are brothers who divided the world up between them. Sir David took television and nature, and Lord Dickie took films and calling people 'darling'. It is a measure of their benevolence as dictators of our hearts that they have never got greedy and breached the terms of their own remit. Sir David has never once forsaken the silverback gorilla to make a longwinded biopic of Charlie Chaplin, and Lord Dickie has constantly refused to step down from the BAFTA stage and stare at a tree frog.

But soon they must retire, and this is good news for you as a Dangerous man because of the job opportunities. What could be more Dangerous than exploring the natural world on HD? Meeting some increasingly Dangerous animals and plants as the public's lust for excitement grows, and then going on to meet some increasingly Dangerous Hollywood producers afterwards? It's a risky life being an Attenborough substitute, but at least it's never boring (unless it's a long-winded biopic of Charlie Chaplin, or another documentary about that other Charlie, Charles Darwin, inventor of the monkey).

EVEL KNIEVEL AND EDDIE KIDD

Because they are essentially the same person. Knievel was, as his name suggests, a bit more evil (although in all the banks and trains he jumped over he never shot nobody), while Eddie Kidd, being British, was clearly the more talented. Proof? Jumping over an AMERICAN single-decker bus is by definition twice as easy as jumping over a British double-decker.

Copying either of these is very easy. Just take your motorbike to the middle of any busy town, take it to the roof of any large building and wait for the rush hour. Soon a big line of static buses will form and you'll be able to jump over them. Warning, though: they will be lengthways buses.

JEREMY CLARKSON

He's real, in a way. And a lot easier to emulate, because he only does two things. One is making provocative right- wing statements a lot like a funny *Daily Express* – health and safety, women, traffic, all that – which to be honest isn't very dangerous in Britain because lots of people agree with that completely seriously and all the people who don't can't do anything about it because they're too weak from living on celery and water and writing to the *New Statesman*. The other

What happens when you cross Stirling Moss with Margaret Thatcher.

isn't that Dangerous but it is a lot of fun. He seems to spend most of his life in Germany talking to a camera mounted on his wing mirror. When he's not doing that he has fun smashing things up and driving very fast in eye-wateringly expensive cars over some salt flats. This only looks Dangerous. When there is something really life-threatening, one of his younger 'colleagues' (or 'employees', as the BBC calls them) takes over.

The catch here, of course, is that you need an enormously powerful back-up organisation (or 'BBC', as the BBC calls itself) behind you to do all these things. This is why other presenters on other TV channels just find themselves driving around British airfields at 40 miles an hour. In all probability, you do not even have your own television show, which means that if you want to do a Clarkson you'll find that if you crash or get a ticket or undermine social democracy you'll get banged up or have to have your broken neck treated on the NHS. Which would be ironically droll.

STEVE IRWIN

Best not.

GUY FAWKES

England's most exciting Catholic since Thomas More, except he killed fewer people, Guy Fawkes is such a mensch that he gave us the word 'guy', meaning 'Man'. He also gave us Bonfire Night, which if you're American or under 40 is like Halloween only a lot better, because you get bonfires and fireworks and free soup. Fawkes is innately Dangerous, being a would-be terrorist and someone who'd be great at a fireworks display, at least until he asked you what the dummy on the fire was meant to be. Imitate Guy Fawkes any way you want and it would be Dangerous, although we feel duty-bound to point out that, regrettably, blowing up Parliament is illegal. Cheap shot!

GEORGE BEST

Again, very good at two things. Kicking a ball, and going out with beautiful women while drunk. Whichever of these options you pick says a lot about what kind of man you are.

The ultimate male role model, which is why God invented women, for health and safety reasons.

LORD NELSON (VERSUS LORD WELLINGTON)

They met, you know. Wellington was unimpressed with Nelson, who he clearly thought was a bit of a nonce. But then Nelson turned it round and charmed the Iron Duke, so he clearly is the best. In fact, there's nothing that's not the best about Nelson, who was cooler in every way than Wellington. He probably won more battles than Wellington, and while Nelson never got to be Prime Minister, Wellington was a very unpopular PM. In fact, Wellington was not called 'The Iron Duke' as one might suppose because of his successful rout of the Emperor Napoleon at Waterloo, nor indeed because he was made of iron, but because he was so disliked by his countrymen that he had to have iron shutters fitted to his windows to stop them throwing bricks at him while he was having his breakfast. But more importantly, Wellington's love life is of no consequence, whereas Nelson was at it like knives all day long. And he looked great, and he had better wounds than Wellington, who just had a big nose, which doesn't count.

Copying Lord Nelson is harder now, as the Navy frowns on pretending you can't read signals. Although it is a lot more lenient nowadays on admirals telling other men to kiss them.

MARY SEACOLE

She's very now, you know, and rightly so. Lots of people in the right-wing so-called press have had a go at top Crimean War nurse Mary Seacole's recent rise to fame, claiming that she's only now being seen as a British hero because she was Afro-Caribbean. This is rubbish. Mary Seacole is great because she was like Florence Nightingale (who hated her) only about a million times better. Where Nightingale just moped around, sponging soldiers and waving her lamp, Mary Seacole ran pubs in the Crimea as well as healing the sick. So that's Mary Seacole 1, Florence Nightingale 0.

It's easy to emulate Seacole as loads of British people run pubs in hot countries, but harder if you do it properly and open a pub in a war zone. But hey, surely even the Taliban enjoy a pint now and then.

EDDIE 'THE EAGLE' EDWARDS

He had the last laugh, you know. He might not have been a great athlete (although it must be said that clearly he was better than most of us, as we have not been picked to represent our country in big sports) and his single was rather poor, but Eddie retains our hearts for ever and still gets to go on talk shows and meet Lily Allen, a fate seemingly denied to Tim Henman and other less interesting sports figures.

Eddie's life was a dangerous one, with all that skiing and soaring into the skies, so be careful if you fancy copying it. You might want to cut out the middle man here and go straight on to the part where you go on talk shows and meet Lily Allen. And don't worry if the host asks you what you're famous for: these days guests for talk shows are chosen from the electoral roll, like jurors. Next time it could be you.

EWAN McGREGOR AND CHARLES 'CHARLIE' BOORMAN

Jesus. Dear God. Oh hell. These are just some of the expressions that come to mind whenever Ewan McGregor and his lackey Charles 'Charlie' Boorman appear on our screens. Two men in early middle age with motorbikes and a dream – to ride around Europe on their motorbikes, or around Africa on their motorbikes, or around Asia on their motorbikes, or around America on their motorbikes. Listen to them as they sit by the campfire after riding around Europe or Africa, or Asia or America on their motorbikes, engaging in the kind of banter that normally indicates repressed homosexuality or just a belief that not being funny is funny! The whole thing is massively pointless and if Ewan McGregor wasn't so nice-looking with his beard, nobody would watch – a fact borne out when McGregor had to go and actually make some films, leaving 'Charlie' to travel around the world on his own.

You cannot easily emulate Ewan McGregor, although mumbling in a fawn dressing gown will help, but it's very simple to emulate Charles 'Charlie' Boorman. All you need is . . . well, nothing really. Oh, and as for the Dangerous part – well, if you want to go round Borneo talking like a dick, good luck.

AMY WINEHOUSE

Can there be a better role model for the Dangerous person than Amy Winehouse? In an age where male rock stars have proven to be disappointingly anodyne, with their personal trainers and their career strategies, Amy stands out like a proud symbol of hope for popular music. What do U2 do after a show? They watch a video of their own performance, seeking to improve it. One doubts that Ms Winehouse is able to watch a house after one of her shows, let alone a video. What does Chris Martin do on tour? He spends time with his wife and children. Again, Amy wins; she spends time with people unable to speak. And she is so much cooler than Pete Doherty, who insists on ruining his cool slacker image by releasing rather feeble albums. Amy appears to have drawn the line at two albums, giving herself more free time to be completely off her head.

Copying Amy Winehouse is tricky, because not only do you have to have the finest soul voice of your generation but also you might actually die. You can wimp out and copy Doherty (can't sing, falls over a lot) but why not set the bar high? She is the Janis and Jimi and Jim of the modern age and if she could register us doing it, we would salute her.

IGGY POP

Like Amy Winehouse only calmer, Iggy Pop is another excellent role model for the Dangerous person. Iggy has had the kind of life most of us can only dream about, and then wake up hoping that it *was* only a dream. He was born James Jewel Osterburg in 1947, the son of a troll and a construction worker (some of these facts may be imprecise) and became the lead singer of The Stooges, a band famous for dressing either as Nazis or not dressing at all. Iggy's stage act has at various times included one or more of the following: nudity, self-mutilation, being drugged out of his mind, walking on the audience's hands, all of the

Named after, and now starting to resemble, an iguana.

above all at the same time and, most frighteningly, crooning.

Iggy's life is so extreme that at one point he was bailed out of a mental hospital by David Bowie, which in the 1970s must have been like having The Joker as a character witness. But his subsequent career has seen him enjoy both chart success and critical respect and, most recently, become the spokesperson for an insurance policy. As a Dangerous (Post) Middle-Aged Man, Iggy Pop is a great man. Rudyard Kipling might have had Iggy in mind when he wrote: 'If you can do all this and hold you head up high/ Or even at all/ I'll be amazed, my son.'

CLIFF RICHARD

That said, rock'n'roll, as the Americans call the music industry, perhaps wishing it was 1957 and everyone still cared what they thought, is a safe and predictable place if you wish to lead an exotic lifestyle. There are very few jobs where massive drug abuse is not frowned on – the City of London, perhaps, and teaching – but rock'n'roll isn't one of them. So in a job where sex and drugs and bad behaviour are encouraged, and if you don't do them you're a freak, perhaps we should acknowledge the bravery and sheer Dangerousness of Cliff Richard, a man who has retained both his drug virginity and his actual virginity in the face of all the gak and shagging a man could ask for. Cliff, you are, in context, the most Dangerous man in the world.

CHAPTER 11

LIAISONS DANGEREUSES

Pretty Dangerous. The soul singer who sang 'No romance without finance' was not being excessively cynical. It's all very well throwing away your past life on a big sexy whim and saying 'Hang the future, I'm ready for love' if you've got a few million in the bank. For the rest of us, it's a bit like saying 'Hang food and drink, I'm going to live off air for the rest of my life.' It may be possible and there are a few weird people who claim to have done it, but in all honesty it's not going to happen.

Picture the scene: you look around you at the possibly slightly grey and grim scene that is your life. Something is cooking in the kitchen that makes your taste buds want to hide behind your tongue. Teenagers are making demands of you that would cause a 1970s hijacker to blush. On the table are a selection of bills which surely should have been directed to Caligula's house on the occasion of his stag night. Your own home is falling down in a way which should merit its free destruction by a sympathetic council but instead seems to demand ever-increasing sums of money on your part to prop it up. You yourself, when you accidentally pass a mirror, look like Mike Yarwood doing a fairly poor impression of your dad.

There is, however, a glimmer of light. A young lady at your place of work or your local book club or just, all right, someone you saw from the top of a bus and thought looked quite nice has recently smiled at you, possibly by accident, but that's not the point. Love, the ephemeral flame, has briefly sparked in your breast like a faulty grill. Next to love blossoms hope and, next to those two, sex. None of these things are rational or sensible or will help you with your mortgage things, but they are there and they are exciting and they could change your life.

You leap to your feet, tell the kids to bugger off, leave a note for the wife which tries to sum up thirty years of marriage in ten words but the biro runs out after DEAR, and leave the house. Pausing only to trade in the family 'run'-about for a brand new sports car, you park outside the home of your new beloved and wait . . . Moments later she comes running down the path, breathless in her nightgown, and says –

'What the hell are you doing , you weirdo? I thought the restraining order was working! Go on, sod off out of it before I set my boyfriend on you!'

You drive your brand new sports car into a layby, pull up the hood, and wonder if the previous owner has left any Polos in the glove compartment, and if so, how long a middle-aged man can live on a half a packet. After all, they're mostly air.

REORIENTING YOUR SEXUALITY

There are among our acquaintance one or two perfectly burly, manly, testosteroney men who have – perhaps in order to be even more burly and manly – forsaken sex and romance with women. They are, in short, gay and loving it. And, most

79

Some gay men, cruisin'.

interestingly, a few of these men did not 'come out' as gay until they reached the cusp of middle age. This proves the validity of the Dangerous Middle-Aged Man as a lifestyle, because these men, unlike many of us, are not sitting at home wondering vaguely if they might be able to face another repeat of *CSI* before going to bed with a Harry Potter secretly wrapped in the cover of a Dan Brown novel.

These men are, in short, not living the dull mid-life of a middle aged man. They are, in their own words, Living La Vida Bloke-a. They are, in a tight little nutshell, the archetypal Dangerous Men, doing what most men would want to do, except more so. They are out every night – having no wife and kids to demand their return at nine p.m. – drinking and listening to music until at some point they get bored, down a vast amount of thrilling drugs and then find someone to have sex with. Then they go home to their really, really nice houses, have a kip and the next day spend a few hours doing a fantastically well paid job before going out and repeating last night all over again.

No wonder it was illegal until 1967. The government were clearly terrified that, if the rest of us found out, we'd all be doing it.

WEIRD SEX

One of the ways in which men of a certain age handle the general sexual ennui that comes to us all is to 'spice it up' a little with weird sex, much in the way that people who are fed up with a diet of pizza and fish and chips like to go out for a curry or a Chinese every so often. The problem with modern life is that everyone has not only got fed up with pizza and fish and chips but has also become bored with curry and Chinese. People, to extend the simile further, are looking for dishes so exotic that these days we're living in a world of Thai food with Argentinian embellishments and a side order of Turkestani veg.

What all this means without the metaphor is that in the olden days men were satisfied with a bit of the other once a week whether they wanted to or not. Now, thanks to the internet forcing pornography into the unwilling, well, fairly willing, maws of most of the world, we have seen what other people have been doing and we want some. Worse, we've tried what other people have been doing and we've become jaded with it – so we want more and weirder. And this is clearly quite Dangerous. There's little risk in getting into bed with a lady and doing what experts call 'it' for five or ten minutes. You may get a little bit out of breath. You may even fall asleep after. But it's fairly safe. You're extremely unlikely to end up hanging from a door jamb with a tie round your neck and a tangerine in your mouth. So think on.

SEX ABROAD

There is an urban myth about the show *Mr and Mrs*, in which married couples were asked questions designed to test how well they knew each other. One young bride is alleged to have been asked, 'Where's the most unusual place you've had sex,' to which she replied . . .*

Anyway, the point of that story is that it's not how you do sex or with whom you do it that can be really Dangerous, it's where you do it. In some countries you can tie a goat to your face, chew on some tangerines and invite most of Man City to join in and you'd probably get a government grant. In others, fairly minor sexual peccadilloes are illegal. The southern states of the USA forbid you to do most things you can see on a T-shirt in Oxford Street and in Saudi Arabia sex on the beach isn't just a cocktail, it's a ~~cocktail~~ severely unpleasant punishment, particularly if you're both drunk and married to someone else.

Should you fancy some Dangerous sex and be limited by your budget, don't worry! Experience tells us that you can get into trouble just as easily in your parents' front room. Especially if enough time has passed and they are now in an old people's home.

* 'Up the bum.'

CHAPTER 12

FATAL FEMALES

More specifically, Dangerous women to go out with. We should define our terms still further here as you don't want to misinterpret the phrase 'Dangerous women' as referring to axe murderesses. No doubt Lizzie Borden always had a good story at dinner parties, but she's not someone you'd feel comfortable with on a Sunday afternoon jaunt to B&Q ('No, darling, let's just look at the bathroom fittings . . . no, put down that . . . AARGH'). By Dangerous women we also don't mean the likes of (insert name of famous gold-digger here) whose character and reputation is spotless as far as we can see but whose history indicates a certain propensity to marry increasingly rich men and later divorce them for sums that everyone except the rich men might consider eminently reasonable. There is Danger in life and there is the rolling inevitability of watching your wallet explode in your face. You're after a trophy girlfriend, not a girlfriend after your trophies.

Axe murderesses and gold-diggers aside, there are some fantastically Dangerous women out there, some of whom seem to share a penchant for intercontinental adoption and some of whom don't. Some are conventionally beautiful and some are not. It takes all kinds of women to make a Dangerous world, and that is by and large a good thing. From Mata Hari to Heather Mills, Dangerous women have introduced different kinds of risk, edginess and on occasion sheer bloody terror to the lives of men. Glamour is often part of the Danger, but it need not be. Let us take you by the hand now, and lead you into a world of Dangerous Love . . .

LARA CROFT

Quite possibly the ultimate Dangerous Woman for the Dangerous Middle-Aged Man. The opposite of, say, *The Simpsons'* Marge Simpson, Lara Croft is an archetypal figure of excitement and desire for men of a certain age who really don't get out enough. Attractive, physical, intelligent (she wears glasses, well, all right, sunglasses), Lara Croft is an expert in archaeology – although her digs do seem to be pursued rather amateurishly as normal archaeologists favour entering areas of historical interest with little brushes and trowels rather than high-powered handguns and grenades – and adventurous. She is also very attractive, so you'd want to go on those life-threatening adventures with her. The only problem here, of course, is that she doesn't exist and the only way you'll ever get to interact with her is to play a video game featuring her name, or – and this is a very good Next-Best Thing – hang out with the real Lara Croft, aka –

ANGELINA JOLIE

Angelina Jolie is both sultry and mysterious in the great Mata Hari tradition, and comes along with a hint of Danger in her make-up. And this is not just because she plays bad girls in films but because she appears to be a genuinely exciting person. You'd never know as you sat there reading the paper over breakfast while Angelina sat opposite you polishing her guns over muesli what the day would hold in store for you both. Perhaps Angelina would rush you off to get a love tattoo in some Balinese bordello. Maybe she'd fly you to the African continent to adopt another child. Possibly she'd insist that it was your turn to do the dishes as she did them last night. The whole idea is a fantastically Dangerous roller coaster of possible love. Plus she comes with the added edge of alienating all your female friends who can't forgive her for stealing Brad Pitt away from the lovely Rachel from *Friends*.

Would any of this world be yours? There's really no way of knowing unless you take the plunge and write to what must surely be her real account on Facebook and demand a date.

GWYNETH PALTROW

In many ways the Anti-Jolie, Gwyneth Paltrow enjoyed a respectable career as a rising star in Hollywood for several years until something terrible happened and she was seduced by Christian-acting 'rock' star and Coldplay front man Chris Martin. Since then she has gone from being a winsome starlet to a sort of slightly hippieish figure who called her firstborn child Apple and refuses to talk about her husband in interviews, probably because she knows we would all implode from boredom.

Yet we believe that underneath this prim exterior beats the heart of a woman who demands a more exciting lifestyle. We suggest that you unleash this better Paltrow. The easiest way would be to pose as an importer of Fair Trade coffee products or the promoter of a vague benefit concert for something fuzzy and Third World, and organise a meeting with Ms Paltrow and Mr Martin. Then, having introduced yourself, shoot Chris Martin in the leg and declare your undying love for Gwyneth. She will in all probability be so touched by your devotion and – more likely – so relieved to have found an escape from her stultifying life that she will run away and live on a speedboat with you.

BETH DITTO

The singer with modernist disco band The Gossip, Beth Ditto is a splendidly Dangerous woman, not least because as a bisexual woman who has no qualms about being not exactly a size nine, she clearly does not give a fig for convention. Which means that you're in with a chance, especially if you've got more conversation than the besotted lipstick lesbians who attend Gossip concerts just so they can shout, 'We love you, Beth!' during the quiet bits. Again, finding a moment to tell Beth who you are may prove difficult with her dizzy lifestyle of parties, fashion shoots and rock festivals but chances are she'll be so delighted by your persistence (and belief that because you're both about the same weight you were born to be together) that she'll agree to go out with you for a pint.

MADONNA

The template for the Dangerous Woman, Madonna is now, like you, over 40. Unlike you, she is in superb physical shape, has seen off two husbands and, despite her penchant for Third World adoptions, is still clearly able to stand up for herself in any situation. One imagines that if Planet Earth were attacked by some hideous huge aliens, President Obama would wait until all other options had been exhausted and then say, 'OK, send in Madonna,' and then Earth would be saved. But at what cost? Why not throw her a love note wrapped around one of your shoes at the next Madonna concert and find out? You won't regret it, possibly.

Madonna, 'playing the guitar'.

KATIE PRICE

The fact that for many years she traded under a different name – Jordan, if you were out – is just one of the reasons that from time to time Ms Price resembles a classic super villain. As Jordan, she was the Dangerous 'glamour model' whose photo shoots and videos might have portrayed her as a lust-crazed bimbette with no self-control, yet whose financial success and self-management skills reveal her as something much more Dangerous – a one-woman financial empire who is both News International AND Rupert Murdoch rolled into one person. As Katie Price, she is a slightly less humorous person who still seems to prefer the company of horses to people. Either way, as the former pop star Peter Andre has recently found out to his well-publicised chagrin, Katie/ Jordan would be an extremely Dangerous person to go out with. We suggest you approach her with a diamond ring and a very solid business plan.

STELLA RIMINGTON

The real-life Dame Judi Dench, Stella Rimington was the first female head of M15 and is therefore not only extremely cool and something of a celeb, but one of the few people on this list who could have all your enemies vanish in the night. Except, possibly, for Madonna.

(HAPTER 13

UNSAFE SEX

There used to be a book or a film called *30 Is A Dangerous Age, Cynthia*, which, despite having the kind of snappy title that multiplex kids go for, actually came out in the 1960s. As a title, that might have been true back in them days but frankly in the modern age this is complete nonsense. 30-year-olds these days have it easy. They have lots of money, lots of sex, lots of downloads and they spend all day dressed like wealthy children in T-shirts with pictures of ghetto blasters and kids' TV-series icons of the 1980s all over them. So balls, frankly, to 30-year-olds, and balls to Cynthia while we're at it.

The most Dangerous age is of course middle age, as we're sure you are aware; but what is the most Dangerous thing about middle age? It used to be things like running out of tobacco for your pipe, or wondering if your son had remembered to bring you a copy of *Railway Modeller* on his six-monthly visit. But in this thrilling brave new millennium the most Dangerous thing about being a middle-aged man is – sex!

Middle-aged men of the olden days were generally untroubled by sex. Unless they were clearly over-stimulated figures like the President of France or Oscar Wilde, every man in the world over 40 was about as interested in sex as his lady wife was. While, admittedly, artistic types like Philip Larkin or Mick Jagger might occasionally order up something wrapped in a plain brown envelope (Larkin) or flown in from a sex farm in Hungary (not Larkin), all the other middle-aged men were more concerned with the problem of the garden gnome by the pond needing a new fishing rod than with the state of their own, as it were, fishing rods.

But times have changed. Sexual intercourse began for poor old mail-order-porn poet Larkin in 1963, around the time of the Beatles' first LP, and therefore too late for him. Today's middle-aged men, who were born, never mind after the release of any of the Beatles' LPs but even after the release of the Beatles' solo LPs, even *Wings Over America*, have a very different attitude to sex. Namely, they want it.

Another poet, John Betjeman, famously declared shortly before he died that his main regret in life was, 'not having had more sex', but he was, obviously, quite old at the time so it was a bit late for him. The modern middle-aged man is determined not to make the same mistake as John Betjeman and aims to have as much sex as possible, preferably with over-stimulated young ladies who are from foreign lands where they like doing it. Naturally, this can cause something of a problem, because most middle-aged men are married, or 'in a relationship' (which seems not to be the same thing, as though getting married effectively ends your relationship with your partner). And in Western society that can cause problems, especially with one's wife or 'partner' who might not be entirely amenable to the Middle-Aged Man going out and getting jiggy with half of Czechoslovakia.

Also, today's middle-aged man is not the free-love hippie of the 1960s or the sideboarded swinger of the 1970s. No professorship in sociology for him, nor membership of an enormously successful rock group. Even that dubious concept the 'open marriage' has proved to be about as effective as that similar idea, the 'open sandwich', i.e. one false move and all the good stuff falls out. It's just not that easy to be a Dangerous-Sex Man nowadays. Women are far less gullible, almost as much so as their lawyers, and lawyers add a level of danger to any situation.

Open Marriage.   *Open Sandwich.*

But when the sap is rising bad thoughts crowd out all sanity. Which means that now, like a dad taking a son to one side to look at some rabbits, it is time for us to take you aside and say, like 1980s rappers Salt-N-Pepa – let's talk about sex. More specifically, all the good things and the bad things you can be.

THE AU PAIR

They're probably not called that any more, are they? They were called that because once upon a Seventies, all *au pairs* were French, and pouting, and somewhat murky on the extent of their duties – should they be putting the children to bed, or their employer? Later this ambiguity was resolved by the introduction of Swedish *au pairs*, who had no problem letting the kids scream themselves hoarse while daddy poured them a Blue Nun, and James Last did the rest.

Nowadays middle-aged men should be advised to be careful, because – putting aside the moral issues for a moment – there are two major Dangers with the modern *au pair*, or Live-In Child Care Assistant. One is that she doesn't really love you, and so at the heart of your affair is a cold stone like, say, a diamond that she saw in a shop that was quite cheap, considering. And the other is that she might actually love you, in which case you are utterly stuffed, because today's *au pair* comes from a very tightly-knit family in the foothills of somewhere, a family who not only believe that love should be commemorated in a complex ceremony involving goat's blood and crying, but also that when you marry one family member, you marry all of them, even the ones who are bringing unskilled labour into Watford by lorry.

If you must go for the *au pair* option, make sure you get everything in writing first; she won't be offended and will even be actually impressed as her lawyers have already drawn up a draft agreement outlining the exchange of sex, money, travel and diamonds that are quite cheap, considering. Or hire a hitman. While against the spirit of romance in many ways, again this is something her folks back home can respect, as for them assassination is part of the very concept of 'family'.

THE AFFAIR

Perhaps the *au pair* option is not for you. Maybe you are not so much a creature of impulse that you don't fall for the first beautiful woman you see smoking a cigarette when she should be ironing the sheets. Maybe you've even spoken to women outside the house from time to time, and have met girls in the office, or at the shops, or picking up the kids from school (this last is very Dangerous, as one day your kids will utter the deadly phrase, 'We have a home mummy and an after-school mummy.')

If you're going to go out with a woman who is neither your wife nor your Live-In Care Assistant, then this is called an Affair. Affairs are the centrepiece, the beating heart and mind of Dangerous Life, as they involve the following genuinely thrilling things:

ASSIGNATIONS

You'd think that texting and emails would remove the danger from affairs, what with them making it easier for you to get in touch with your illicit bunk-up. But this is not so; because back in the old days when making an assignation meant delivering letters via a small boy that would then be thrown into the fire (the letters, obviously, not the small boy) or leaving a cryptic soap-powder box in the window (OMO – Old Man Out), things were much more secret as there was less of a paper trail. Nowadays, it's terrifically Dangerous. Mobile phones are left around. Emails can be retrieved. And, if you're a really careless Dangerous Middle-Aged Man, you might suddenly remember that you've agreed to take part in a reality TV show and a camera crew has been following you around for the past six months.

So the choice is yours: be foolishly Dangerous and use modern media to arrange your assignations, or be old school, and set a lantern 'pon your sill afore thou goest to bed. Tell your partner it's an eco-friendly gesture and you might even get away with it.

BIJOU LOVE NESTS

The Victorians, we're often told, were utterly strait-laced and never had sex, unless it was with a piano leg. In reality, they were at it like knives twenty-four hours a day, which explains all the children. Clearly seventy years of sexual repression cannot merely find an out in marital sex, as Charles Dickens proved after he fathered several children on his good lady wife, and then – in classic male menopausal fashion – traded her in for a younger model.

What he did next was much better; he observed one of the finer traditions of the nineteenth century and established his mistress in what used to be called a bijou love nest. These were generally to be found in leafy Saint John's Wood, a part of London which in those days was absolutely crawling with mistresses who would all get up about noon, accept a cup of tea from their maid, and then lounge about in revealing underwear until the head of a prosperous ironworks or similar turned up after work to relieve them of their lacy French garters. Life could go on for years like this, until both the head of the ironworks and the mistress were too old to care and both headed off into separate seaside retirements, one in Ramsgate and the other in Deauville.

We say that this system should be revived today, especially

in an era where property prices are up and down like a Victorian mistress's drawers. Installing a mistress is not only fairly economical but in a perfect world could be tax deductible. It also avoids issues like second marriages and internet dating. Perhaps a company like Barratt, the inventor of the otherwise pointlessly small house, could be incentivised by the government into providing bijou love nests for saucy mistresses? It would certainly be a measure popular in Parliament.

CHAPTER 14

DIVORCE

The most risky activity of the lot for middle-aged men, divorce beats skydiving with lead weights instead of parachutes, being a human crash-test dummy or spending a year as Gordon Brown's stunt double for all-out, no-holds-barred, world-class, ocean-going, seeing-eye, gripping-hand Dangerousness. Why? Because Divorce is the polar opposite of Sex, which can be dangerous but is great. Divorce is dangerous and it is not great. If sex is the most fun you can have with your clothes off, then divorce is the least fun you can have with your clothes on. If sex is only good when it's dirty, then divorce is only bad when it's dirty. Lots of people practise making love on their own; nobody practises getting divorced on their own. Because it's horrible. Not only is it horrible, but it's not horrible in an exciting, short sharp shock way like being shot in the head. Divorce is horrible in a slow, grinding, never-ending depressing way, like being sent to boarding school with a gang of Easter Island statues who have decided to bully you.

As a Dangerous Middle-Aged Man you are of course in the demographical area where you are incredibly likely to get divorced, because babies and children can't, teenagers can't

Yeah, but think of the make-up sex.

be bothered to get married, old people have decided to stick it out, and that just leaves a few people in their 20s and 30s who like being married . . . for now. So what we're saying is that divorce is a) almost certainly inevitable and b) almost certainly your fault. Time, then, to plan for this slow, grey, grinding tidal wave of fear and misery. Time to make divorce both Dangerous and Fun.

DIVIDING STUFF UP

Dividing stuff up is one of the worst parts of divorce, as suddenly you and your ex discover that both of you cannot live without the tea towels of the Isle of Wight or the toaster that doesn't really work but that's not the point, I love that toaster and you know it. And dividing stuff doesn't really work – you can't put your Gary Numan CDs on the floor and palm off the moody ballads on your ex and keep the snappy fast numbers for yourself. There is of course a solution to this issue, first propounded in the 1960s sitcom *Steptoe And Son* where they fall out and put a wall down the middle of the house. And while that failed, being fiction, there is a way to make it work, which is to think of it not as a petty division between two unhappy people, but to see the origins of this plan.

Because the whole wall-down-the-middle business is of course based on very large historic divorces, such as that of East and West Berlin. As a strategy it's one that would save a lot of heartbreak in the long run, especially if you think of yourself and your ex not so much as North and South Korea, say, but Roman-occupied England and Pictish Caledonia, or China and Mongolia. Seeing yourselves as two mighty warrior nations who can no longer share a border safely without carrying out raids to, for example, reclaim the remote control or hold her complete set of Gary Numan CDs hostage, can be helpful for your self-esteem.

We're saying really go for it. Who needs the dull trauma of drawing up documents about who gets what and then paying some lawyer to repeat what you just said to another lawyer when you can just hire a builder to come in and knock up a nice brick wall running through the entire house – leaving, of course, a heavily mined no man's land or buffer zone between the kitchen and the downstairs toilet. There will inevitably be casualties – your ex-wife's attractive air stewardess friends, who were visiting from France, may have found themselves in the kitchen as the wall went up, and consequently are trapped forever in your part of the house. Likewise, the letter box, through which all the bills come into the house, may somehow be on her side of the wall. The back garden may be bisected in such a way as to have the barbecue and the shed on your side and the compost heap on hers. These things happen and they cannot be prevented.

AVOIDING LAWYERS

Lawyers cause heartbreak. We're not saying – because some lawyers might sue us – that lawyers set out to cause heartbreak. We're not claiming, if anyone asks, that the bastards wake up each morning and think to themselves, 'What a lovely day, I can't wait to get in the office and ruin some poor sod's life, for money.' And we're certainly not suggesting that they then get in the shower and sing, 'I love ruining people's lives!' at the top of their fine baritone voices. Because lawyers are people too, and it's not their fault that they couldn't get work with Amnesty International or the Citizens' Advice Bureau or any number of bodies who ceaselessly strive to make the world a better place and are in dire need of more help. No. We respect lawyers' rights as much as the next person who has been sued for libel in the High Court. So please, lawyers, bear all that in mind when we say that Dangerous Middle-Aged Men can avoid a lot of heartbreak when they seek to dissolve their marriages using intermediaries other than lawyers. And don't take us to court.

Lawyers do spend a lot of their time essentially delivering messages from one ex-partner to the other. You could just cut out the middle man here by talking to each other yourself. You could send emails and meet up and all that but not only is that not Dangerous, but you might find that you get on with each other again, and where's the fun in that? Why not add some Dangerous spice to the split up by hiring small, inky-fingered boys to do the messaging? Imagine how much more fun your ex's day will be when, instead of receiving a dull letter from a lawyer, she opens the door to find a grubby urchin who shouts, "'E wants the juicer, miss!' and then runs away laughing to play ducks and drakes in a nearby rainy gutter. You too can experience a parallel thrill when, dozing in front of *Top Gear* in the evening, you are awakened by your front window being smashed by a brick with a message tied round it that reads 'YOUR NOT GETTING THE DEE VD PLAYER'.

Or if that's too cosy, why not hire ninjas? We've seen them in films so they must exist. Instead of having messages delivered, pay some ninjas to transport your ex to a remote Japanese castle where your demands will be delivered by a trained assassin. It's certainly a lot more interesting than spending the morning in a solicitor's warm waiting room. Engage the services of a sky-writing firm so that everyone can enjoy the fun when she wakes up to see the words NOBODY LIKES YOUR MOTHER trailed across the sky – but be careful! Two can play at that game, and you don't want half the town to gaze into the heavens and see clouds of smoke telling the world that YOUR WINKIE COULD NOT SATISFY AN AMOEBA.

KEEPING THE KIDS

Hopefully at this time in your life, any children you have will be old enough not to be too deeply hurt by the divorce. If they are teenagers, in fact, they'll be quite pleased, as all their mates at school have divorced parents and they were feeling left out. Having married parents at all these days is like growing up as one of the Plymouth Brethren: you feel like a throwback to a more primitive, peculiar era, and school bullies will thump you on your parents' wedding anniversary.

So don't worry – you're not being selfish as you neglect your kids for another business trip to Paris to satisfy your middle-aged lust on Martika from Human Resources, you're helping your children fit in with their peer group.

Of course, because they're not strictly adults yet, you may find that after the divorce they will still insist on living with at least one of you. This is obviously a bit selfish because there is only one good thing about getting divorced. Two words – 'bachelor pad'. No matter how squalid or luxurious your first post-marital home is, it's clearly not going to be improved by the presence of a couple of whingeing adolescents who don't see how you playing all your New Order albums in chronological order is going to get their school lunches made any faster.

Your ex is a smart cookie and she has found many reasons not to get the kids; perhaps she is already with a new partner, who finds children 'restrictive'. Perhaps she has got a new life, travelling the world and getting smashed on what was once partly your money. Perhaps she has simply moved without giving you her address. In any case you will find yourself in the annoying position of being a Dangerous Middle-Aged Man with a couple of frankly adventure-limiting human albatrosses in tow. Something must clearly be done. After all, once upon a time children did not so much fly the nest as get kicked out as soon as possible.

A few Dangerous suggestions, then, on ensuring that you are not lumbered with the offspring:

PLEAD YOUR CASE IN LAW

Everybody wants to keep their kids. That's the assumption judges make. Day in and day out, it's the same old story: we want to keep the kids. So the sheer novelty of a parent arguing *against* having their children living with them must surely impress the courts? Think how delighted they'd be to get such an unexpected case! Imagine if you won, and how many other harassed would-be newbie bachelor dads would be eternally grateful for this lessening of their financial and emotional burden! Warning: your kids may not see things the same way and you may spend your dotage living out of bins because of this one Dangerous act.

JOIN FATHERS FOR JUSTICE

Fathers for Justice has always struck us as a pretty fun kind of thing to join. You get lots of Grade A Dangerous fun – climbing tall buildings and national monuments, dressing up as superheroes, and being on the telly a lot. The only downside is the rather dull message conveyed by these people: something to do with access to children or financial payments, we're not entirely sure. Nevertheless, one fact that everyone knows about kids, particularly teenagers, is that they absolutely hate to be embarrassed. And what could be more embarassing for any teenager than a father who not only spends his time climbing Nelson's Column dressed as the Green Lantern but also tells everyone that he is *doing it for his children*. The phrase 'OMG I AM SO EMBARRASSED!' was clearly invented for just such an occasion.

It all makes perfect sense: if you want to have Dangerous fun, avoiding the police and climbing big things while at the same time unfolding a clever plan to keep the kids away from you, then this is the way to go. Best of all, your kids will in later life feel really guilty and make sure that you have a super keen place to live in your extreme old age.

'Nigel! Get down from there!'

JUST SAY TO HELL WITH IT, COME LIVE WITH ME, KIDS

This is a very risky strategy because they might accept. There is a faint – a very faint – chance that, being teenagers, they won't want to live with the parent who has for the past decade and a half cooked for them, cleaned for them, ironed their clothes and made sure they get to school, and will instead opt for the parent who has done nothing but teach them how to swear and belch more effectively. So by inviting your kids to live with you, you are playing with fire. If you do take this highly Dangerous approach, which is a bit like playing Russian Roulette with your future, set out your stall like this: clean your bachelor pad from floor to ceiling. Throw out Martika from Human Resources and that man you met in the pub who claimed to have some legal space vodka. Hide all your gadgets and your magazines and your booze. Remove all your furniture. Then invite the kids over and, sitting on a pile of old Yellow Pages, say, 'Children, I have decided to renounce my old ways for a life of Christian poverty. Please move in with me and join my six-week prayer marathon.' Then bless them individually. It is extremely unlikely they will ever come around again, and you will be free to live the Dangerous party life until your liver too asks for a divorce.

DISREGARD THE CHILD LABOUR LAWS

Put the little beggars to use. Somebody out there must know someone who still employs under-aged labour. Surely our chimneys aren't suddenly sweeping themselves? And thanks to animal-rights groups, pit ponies are no longer allowed to pull coal trucks. Failing any of that, other countries are known to be a lot more lax with their child employment laws than we are. Let the kids in on your new exciting lifestyle by taking them to Asia and leaving them outside a sweatshop. After all, if you're a teenager being able to make your own trainers must be the coolest skill in the world.

CHAPTER 15

ROCK 'N' ROLL SUICIDE

Being famous is very dangerous indeed. In fact, the more famous you are, the more dangerous it is, and it seems to be particularly risky for pop stars. Look at Michael Jackson, dead at 50, addicted to painkillers after his head caught fire while filming a soft-drinks commercial. Look at Elvis Presley, dead at 40. Brian Jones, Jimi Hendrix, Janis Joplin, Jim Morrison, Sid Vicious, Kurt Cobain . . . none of them made it to 30. Of course there are exceptions – Keith Richards, for example, and Shane MacGowan, men who we can only presume synthesise drugs and alcohol in their bodies into vitamins and forms of unnatural nutrition – but for most young men and women who get into the music business, death is indeed their Santa Claus. And for those pop stars who survive their 20s and 30s and don't OD or crash their cars, middle age is surely an even riskier time, as fans forget who you are, you get fat, and instead of sitting in a mansion in Bel Air taking drugs with beautiful models, you are running a pub in Rhyl and sometimes you hear your name misremembered as a wrong answer in a pub quiz.

Becoming a pop or rock star is tricky, especially at your age. But Ian Hunter didn't join rock band Mott The Hoople until he was 30, and even then had to wait several years for fame, as did Joe Strummer (28 at the start of his punk career). It's never too late as Rene from Rene and Renate proved, and a host of others. You can even be a studio boffin and never be seen. However, we're not interested in that aspect of your journey; this isn't a drab handbook for wannabe stars. This is a book on how to be a Dangerous Middle-Aged Pop Star. Don't be like Val Doonican, who released an album called *Val Doonican Rocks . . . But Gently.* Join us now as we give you a few tips for living Dangerously in the world of pop.

HAVE A COMEBACK

This is extremely risky for your career and your ego. Various ways to ensure that you never work again include the following:

REDOING YOUR OWN SONG

There's nothing bleaker in a pop star's discography than a date in brackets after a song title, meaning that you've been forced to revisit your own oeuvre, i.e. you have no new songs. Fact; any discography that has at the top, say, *Let's Get Rocking* can only end, literally, in tears when it has at the bottom *Let's Get Rocking '09.*

NOT LOOKING IN THE MIRROR

For God's sake, before some promoter talks you into going back on the road look in the mirror! Has your hair fallen out? Has your stomach increased in size? Do you have any teeth left? Are you dressed like an idiot? If the answers to any of these questions is 'yes', do not go back on the road. Even successful, still-working stars like Paul McCartney and Mick Jagger go to enormous efforts to look cool. Even supposedly ironic musicians like U2 and Radiohead wouldn't dream of leaving the house if they'd acquired a bit of a beer gut, let alone going on a world tour. It's just not worth it.

DOING THE WRONG TOUR

It doesn't matter how much money they're talking, if you're offered a summer season at Bournemouth Winter Gardens or six weeks at Pontins, do not accept. You don't see Sting posters with his picture in the middle of a big star and the words NOW INCLUDES PENSIONERS' MATINEE, do you? More's the pity. These bookings are to be avoided as they are sure indicators that your career is over.

HIRE YOUR CHILDREN

Why not just have your date of birth tattooed on your face? Rock stars who invite their sons and daughters to be band members may well be kindly and thoughtful but it's just telling the world 'We are past it.' When you go and see a band and there's a 30-year-old rocking out on the bass, and he's standing next to his dad, all you can do is work out the age difference. Remember, in rock only Bob Dylan is allowed to be that old. In fact, the Middle-Aged Rock Star should avoid working with anyone more than five years younger than them. That's you, Tom Jones.

CHANGE DIRECTION

Rock stars who have reached a certain (low) point in their careers often decide to 'inject fresh blood' into their work (unfortunate phrase) by changing their musical direction. Not only does this alienate their few remaining fans, but it also indicates a woeful lack of judgement because most musicians, if we're honest, are only really good at one thing.

The two worst new directions musicians can take, by the way, are going jazz and going young. Going jazz is popular because it means singers who can no longer sing are able to churn out horrible croaky versions of formerly good tunes. Going young is even worse, as some wrinkled old fool stuffs himself into a pair of jeans and a T-shirt and attempts to sing horrible versions of songs by modern cool new bands. This just makes him look like a pervy old dad trying to impress some teenage girls with his knowledge of the charts. That's you again, Tom Jones.

Daughter or collaborator?

And finally, if you really want to risk all, here are some genuinely Dangerous rock-and-roll things to do.

DRINK AND TAKE DRUGS

Obviously. But do remember, you're not as young as you once were. You might try to take a tip from some old rockers, and switch the Jack Daniels for iced tea.

EAT A BAT

It worked for Ozzy Osbourne, who also ate a dove. Find an animal you enjoy eating. No, not chicken.

GET SAMPLED

Amazingly popular as most rap and dance acts seem to be a bit short of new ideas. If by chance you once wrote a catchy riff, these days chances are extremely high that some new act will sample it and you'll get some more money. Best of all is to generously accept their invitation to appear in the video; you'll suddenly acquire all the cool of a Dangerous gangsta-rap combo without having to actually kill anyone.

STEAL SOMEONE ELSE'S SONG

Risky, because you will lose a lot of money, but look at all the publicity George Harrison got when he wrote 'My Sweet Lord' and some lawyers noticed that it had the same tune as 'He's So Fine' by the Chiffons. Harrison also went on to write a song about the court case, so there's artistic inspiration there too.

BE IN THE GENERAL VICINITY OF THE ROLLING STONES

Possibly the most Dangerous thing you can do in the world of rock and pop. Apart from Brian Jones, who drowned in his own pool after being sacked from the band, there's American country rocker Gram Parsons who also OD'd after befriending the band. Mick Jagger's ex-girlfriend Marianne Faithfull became a heroin addict for many years. And Stones fan Meredith Hunter was murdered by Hell's Angels as the Rolling Stones played at the Altamont Festival. You're probably safer playing cricket on a railway line, to be honest.

The Four Horsemen of the Apocalypse:
War, Famine, Plague and Keith Richards.

CHAPTER 16

DESPERATELY STYLISH

The Dangerous Middle-Aged Man by his very nature is cool. You are a Dangerous Middle-Aged Man – you just are *cool.* It's obvious. But being cool is not the same as looking cool. You may have rejected pipe and slippers but even now you're probably embarrassing the living daylights out of your children by dressing like a gangsta rapper and calling the postman 'blood'. This is part of the joy of Dangerous Living: you know that everyone thinks you look ridiculous but as they're the ones who are embarrassed and feeling discomfort and you just think you look fantastic, why should you care? The same applies to dressing as a biker even though you haven't got a motorbike, going 'postcard punk' and getting an absurd novelty-rainbow Mohican, being a White Rasta – surely the most embarrassing look in the history of fashion – and, if you're feeling Dangerously carefree, public nudity. Again, only other people need cover their eyes. You're doing fine.

These days, though, it's hard to stand out in a crowd because the Tribes of Britain are so diverse. Yes, half the country is glumly anonymous in hoodies and trainers, but everyone seems to be a goth or an emo or a member of some other highly decorative group. But don't worry: what these pseudo-individuals have in common is that they are YOUNG and one day most of them will GROW OUT OF IT. You have the advantage over them that you have already grown out of everything that you possibly can grow out of, and if you decide to start looking unusual it will be genuinely threatening because you are a grown man. Here are some tips:

PIERCINGS

With their self-harming associations, piercings bring with them a frisson of Danger. Actually, these days it's not so much a frisson of Danger as a lorryload, because the happy innocent era of doing your ear lobe with a needle and an ice cube is over, and if you want to make any sort of impression on people you pretty much have to put a javelin through your eyelids. The heat is on for piercing fans and you can see the stress in their eyes as they troll about town burdened by increasing amounts of metal covering increasing areas of their bodies. A safety pin through the cheek isn't enough any more; to make even a small impression you have to look as though you've just had your entire head magnetised seconds before running through Rymans.

Fortunately for the Dangerous man, there are ways of

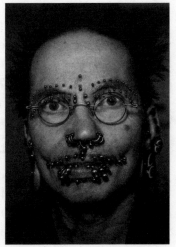

Why not just carry a magnet in your mouth and throw iron filings at your face?

making an impression and upsetting society. Most people who get a piercing or two have them done in very traditionally 'shocking' body zones, namely the face and the genitals. This lends an air of predictability to piercing which you, as a Dangerous Middle-Aged Man can exploit; instead of having bolts and pins shoved into your nostrils and privates, why not get your knees pierced? It's time to boldly pierce where no man has pierced before. You could get your hip pierced while you're at it – thus incurring the gratitude of surgeons in later life.

TATTOOS

Again, not as scary as they used to be. Once upon a time the word MUM in a heart would have been enough to send adults trembling into church to pray for your soul, but recently it's considered perfectly normal to have a vicar who is tattooed from head to toe. Milkmen have floral faces, librarians stamp your books with hands covered in Celtic symbolism, and even your granny is thinking of getting a skeleton on a motorbike for her eightieth. Tattoos are bog common, and this is their Achilles over-decorated heel: they have become genericised. Going to get a tattoo is now as production-line-geared and commercial as going for a burger (although a burger probably stays with you longer than a tattoo and is arguably more toxic). You walk in, you're shown a menu, you pick one, you have it done and you walk outside, feeling a bit special, until you realise that everyone else has had the same tattoo done. You might as well, like some ironists do, have a bar code tattooed on your arm.

There is a way of standing out in this body-adorned world – by designing your own tattoos, tattoos that will anger

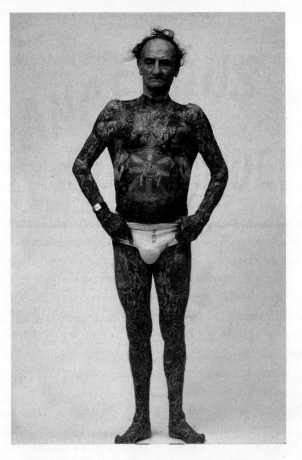

From a distance, he just looks sort of green.

strangers and shock passers-by. How about the face of Anne Widdicombe on your back, or Christine and Neil Hamilton on each bicep? Maybe a nice illustration of Exeter City Centre will express an unusual regional devotion. Or just go for complete and horrifying surrealism and have a picture of your face *tattooed on your own face.*

HAIR

Traditionally, middle-aged men seek to escape convention by growing their hair long, as if to look like rock stars. As rock stars rarely have long hair nowadays and even when they do are still mostly in their 20s, this has the effect of making middle-aged men look, not like famous rockers, but their roadies. There is also the Slide-Down Effect, which is what happens when men with bald patches grow what hair they have left longer and tie it in a ponytail. This doesn't make them look like they've got loads of thick long hair, it makes them look like their hair has slipped off the top of their head and is sliding down their neck towards their back. Not ideal.

The other alternative is almost worse. Many balding men have sought to even things up by shaving all their hair off to avoid the embarrassing middle-aged-man head colour scheme of grey/pink/grey. This is fine and dandy, but means that every pub in the land is now full of heads shining and bristling like lone buttocks in a singles bar. Gone are the days when having a shaved head meant you were either a skinhead or gay, or both.

There's not much you can do about hair, so we recommend – the wig. Wigs are perfect for Dangerous Middle-Aged Men because they are probably the only thing left in the world that is still reviled and hated without any shred of irony. But if you wear one try not to lie and claim that, look, I've still got hair, but instead defy convention and say it loud! I'm bald and proud! This way you'll be doing the right thing. Wigs can look great and, as with everything else in life, the more unnatural the better. Bright colours! Weird cuts! You can do anything!

BODY-HAIR REMOVAL

Not for the weak of spirit. Some of the men we most admire for their physical prowess on the silver screen were almost completely devoid of extraneous body hair. From Tarzan to the Terminator, our fittest and strongest men have shunned body hair, and now that you're at the point in life when the hair that grows most lushly on your body is coming out of your ears, then you should join them. If you're bold enough and sufficiently comfortable with your own sexuality, visit a beauty parlour and ask the attractive lady receptionist to book you in for what is commonly referred to as a 'back, crack and sack' wax. Only the bravest are said to survive this particular male torture which feels like you are having your skin peeled off by a million tiny Velcro-covered scorpions – and that's before they have waxed your scrotum. And why not try doing it competitively amongst like-minded friends? You could have a 'back, crack and sack' race.

CHAPTER 17

EXTREME SPORTS

'Extreme' is very much a sporting buzzword right now, the idea being that normal sports aren't enough but by adding the word 'extreme' you have in effect painted on some go-faster stripes. Thus Extreme Fighting is, well, fightier than any other kind of fighting, whereas Extreme Chess is just chess played by men with bulging veins in their foreheads. If you fancy just looking but not actually being Dangerous you can make yourself look quite fierce just by calling everything you do 'extreme'. Walk into the office with a bag of rackets and tell everyone you're off to play Extreme Badminton. They'll be impressed, if only because they are trying to imagine what the shuttlecocks look like. Only you know that Extreme Badminton is exactly the same as normal badminton, except you frown a lot and grunt more.

Here are a few actual Extreme Sports for you to try your hand at:

'That reminds me, I must defrost the fridge.'

ICE CLIMBING

When rocks just aren't slippery enough . . . ice climbing is exactly what you think it is, i.e. people climbing sheer walls of ice. If you think of it as very slow, vertical ice-skating it seems less tricky but it's definitely not for the faint at heart, or people who've forgotten their gloves.

BMXING

Quite how this one got through the net is something of a mystery, as BMXs are essentially children's bicycles and no matter how many slopes you ride off or how many wheelies you do, you will still look like you have robbed the paper boy. BMXing is fairly dangerous, though, partly because you have to do a lot of risky stunts, and partly because you are far too big for this bicycle and may actually break it.

SNOWBOARDING

Nobody knows (or cares) who the first skateboarder was who took his skateboard to the Alps and, eventually noticing that it didn't work on snow, removed the wheels and turned it into a short fat ski. Whatever the truth is, snow-boarding does seem to be fun. It's pretty risky because you have less control than you do with skis, and also because if you judge people by their clothes, then the people doing it seem to be completely stoned. You really don't want to be going to Sainsbury's after you've smoked a lot of marijuana, let alone be hurtling down the side of an icy mountain on a plank.

BUNGEE JUMPING

Dangerous, yes, and extreme but we're not really sure how this is a sport, because the bungee jumper, unlike the triple jumper or pole-vaulter, has absolutely no control over his actions. Every bungee jumper is surely the same as every other bungee jumper. You just tie some elastic round your ankles and leap off a platform. The only way individual per-formances can vary is if you are fatter than other jumpers or if the elastic is very old. But those circumstances will only mean that you become a bungee plummeter instead.

'The brakes don't woooooork!'

SURFING

The Hawaiians have made at least two great contributions to civilisation. One is the ukulele, and the other is the surfboard. It says a lot about the British character that for many years we favoured the former. There is nothing dangerous about the ukulele, which is why many non-Dangerous Middle-Aged Men were so fond of it. But times have changed and this is the age of the Dangerous Middle-Aged Man. Be proud as you stride out into the waves, surfboard under your arm. Be delighted as you ride the curl or the rip or whatever it's called. But most of all, be astonished that you managed to get into the wetsuit, something that nobody over twenty-five can do with ease.

POLE-VAULTING

This is not officially classed as an extreme sport, perhaps because it's not an activity generally favoured by stoners, but we have included it because of one extraordinary fact: pole-vaulting is actually quite dangerous, with 16 deaths in the last 25 years. It's the mats, apparently.

THE ISLE OF MAN TT RACE

Over 200 people have been killed taking part in this event since it began a century ago. We hesistate to suggest this, but surely much of the controversy over assisted suicide might be avoided if all the people who normally go to Switzerland to end their lives could instead be persuaded to visit the Isle of Man.

CHAPTER 18

FEAR OF FLYING

If God had intended us to fly, the old saying goes, he would not have invented airports. Flying is one of the dullest, grimmest, most unpleasant activities ever invented. There is little doubt that birds wouldn't bother with it if they had to

*Louis Bleriot, the first Frenchman to land
in England and not be shot.*

check in five hours in advance, have their beaks searched and then have their flights cancelled and have to sleep in the airport every time they felt like migrating for the summer. Yet this is the nature of flying in the 21st century.

And the worst of it is, flying is fairly dangerous. Going through the hell of a modern airport just to have your plane plummet into the sea or be hijacked by sky pirates or have its engines filled with auto-asphyxiating geese is somewhat unfair, the aeronautical equivalent of being humiliated several times in a reality pop show only to end up being shot in the head by Cheryl Cole. Dangerous, also, in a boring way. Neither the men nor the flying machines are magnificent nowadays.

So the Dangerous man seeking adventure in the skies is generally well-advised to avoid commercial flights, unless he fancies himself as a hijacker or sky pirate. This certainly has its moments – directing the pilot to fly you to Cuba can produce a visceral thrill – but frankly there are serious flaws. These days, for instance, it's extremely cheap to fly, and if you do hijack a plane you won't be saving that much money but you will almost certainly be shot by the Guardia Naçional when you land. Similarly, if you survive, what are you going to do with a jumbo jet? You can't live in it (the bathrooms are rank) and the chances of selling it on eBay are extremely slender.

So the *Dangerous Book* suggests that you avoid the big airlines if you fancy some cloud-based risk, and instead follow this simple guide to Danger In The Air (and actually follow it, don't just read the paper during the demonstration like you know everything):

It's now been done by an eight-year-old boy.
Should really only be done by eight-year-old boys.

WING WALKING

Contrary to the name, wing walking involves being strapped upright to the centre of a biplane's upper wing and remaining there while it is flown at speeds of up to one hundred miles an hour. This isn't much fun. You could enjoy a similar experience standing up in the back seat of an open-topped car on a motorway. In fact, if that is your idea of fun just ask a chum to drive the brand new Porsche you've squandered your children's university fund on, while you wobble to your feet and imitate that big Jesus statue in Brazil with your arms sticking out while truck drivers throw empty cans of Red Bull at your head. You'll soon realise that your chum is getting the better deal.

If you can bribe an old biplane pilot to take you up, then actual wing walking might be fun – although do remember to ask him not to perform an Immelmann Turn or any other kind of WW1 acrobatic manoeuvre. Best to ask him to fly steady and straight, as though he were bringing home a lot of wrens' eggs. Even then, thinking about it, wind turbulence could be an issue as you slide about, and later off, the wing in your Hush Puppies. In fact, it's probably best to ask him not to take off at all while you just stand on the wing, looking like a scarecrow with an escape plan.

FLYING LESSONS

These are quite normal these days, although – like other things these days – very expensive. So far as we can tell, the only people in Britain qualified to fly their own aircraft are Noel Edmonds and the drummer from Blur. And while this might mean it's easy to get served at the aerodrome club-house bar, it doesn't make for exciting company, unless you are enthralled by conversations about life at Crinkley Bottom, or paradiddles. But what the hell, you're loaded from selling the Porsche and the house and kids, so why not check it out?

Flying your own plane gives you ample opportunities for putting yourself in harm's way. Strong drink always adds a special frisson to piloting; far from safe in the knowledge of where you are, you will be able to fly around completely ratted to your heart's content, occasionally wondering why the sky looks like the M3 only upside down, and if you're lucky you can have a go at that silent film thing where you fly into a barn and come out the other side with your cockpit full of chickens and straw. More likely, you'll never come out, your plane will explode and you and the chickens will burn to death in an enormous straw-powered fireball.

HOT-AIR BALLOONS

Balloons used to have a rather calm, almost dignified vibe to them. Whether it was the Montgolfier Brothers, whose balloons looked like giant Fabergé eggs floating above the fields of Vaux-Le-Vicomte, or that nice woman in the Nimble adverts whose bread was so light it enabled her to slip the surly bonds of Earth, balloons once had a friendly, family image. One thinks of old explorers, gamely flying over the Alps, or young lads escaping from evil barons in children's

Richard Branson – he'll fly in his dangerous balloons but you never see him on one of his rotten trains, do you?

books. But times have changed, and balloons have now acquired a more sinister and, if you will, Dangerous aspect.

The reason for the balloon's new-found infamy is, of course, Richard Branson who, when he was taking time out from running the finest train service the world has ever seen (if the world we're talking about is Mars) used to spend his time hogging the news by flying balloons first around the world and then into the ground. Branson made the words 'balloon' and 'buffoon' synonymous and also ensured that ballooning would always be a bit of a tosser's game.

If you want to be a Dangerous balloonist, your best bet is to adopt the *Enduring Love* model. This film, based on the book by Ian McEwan, teaches us the lesson not only that if you go up in a balloon you will fall out and your body will split into different pieces, but also that if you try and help a balloonist in peril, Rhys Ifans will somehow become your stalker and there will be knives. This is therefore a course riddled with danger, and really, if you want to get yourself into enormous trouble, we say: go and buy a balloon now.

SKYDIVING

Apparently just leaping out of a plane wearing a parachute isn't dangerous enough for some people; they have to actually plummet the hell down towards the Earth like menopausal stones before they pull the ripcord. And not only that, they have to film it, because nothing these days is real unless it's been recorded. And not only *that*, they have to do absurd touchy things like piggybacking, or holding hands, or anything basically which, if it took place on land, would have you marked out as some kind of infantile pervert.

The best way to be dangerous when skydiving is to play

'Wow! This is like Google Earth,
except I've soiled myself.'

Russian Roulette with the parachutes, replacing one of them
with several copies of the *Guardian*. And don't worry too
much about Roger as he hurtles toward the ground with only
the travel section and a Sudoku for company; anyone who
wants to go skydiving probably deserves an early end anyway.

CHAPTER 19

PERIL ON THE SEA

The sea is a cruel mistress, except that you can't have sex with it (no, don't try, you'll get all sand down there) and it doesn't care about lingerie. But what it does care about is being a complete cow. And frankly, you can't blame it. Look at the god it's got: while other gods have winged feet or can turn into bulls or make people fall in love by shooting them, the sea has got Poseidon aka Neptune, who is basically a bad-tempered old man with a fork and a crown who is covered in seaweed. He looks less like a powerful deity ruling his element with wisdom and strength than a tramp who has fallen into the canal.

Perhaps because of its second-rate god, the sea is very much a Dangerous place. From the rock pools crammed with (formerly) clawy crustaceans and poisonous anemones or (nowadays) pollutants to the actual ocean, stuffed with sharks and whales and leviathans, the sea is a scary place. When John Masefield announced 'I must go down to the sea again,' his poetry mates probably went 'Why? It's horrible.'

The sea is the place from which life came. And it's not hard to see why. If you were life, you'd want to get out of the sea as well. It's not safe. The sea is, essentially, the home of drowning. That can't be good. It's also the home of sinking, another activity with very few positive associations. And, most damning of all, it's the home of surfing, and if there's one activity to which idiots are drawn in massive numbers, surfing is it. The only other activity which attracts so many tanned bozos is skateboarding; and surfing is the skateboarding of the sea.

The sea is responsible for other crimes – without the sea, we wouldn't have the awful film *Titanic*, for example – but let's not worry about those now. Suffice to say that for the purposes of the Dangerous Man, there are few places more useful, exciting and dangerous than the sea. In fact, after some discussion, we here at *The Dangerous Book* were unable to come up with any sea-based activities that aren't dangerous. So pull up a deckchair, slide into a rubber ring, and off we go:

DIVING

Just about every form of this insane activity is dangerous on some level. Skydiving, high-board diving, scuba diving, deep-sea diving – none of them have the cosy feeling that you get from sitting in front of the fire toasting muffins, do they? Quite why anybody would want to enter the sea at immense speed when they would be better off approaching it gingerly, like a huge, cold, recently shaved walrus that's regretting its lifestyle choice, is a mystery. But if you want to do something dangerous, diving is your man. Perhaps the most Dangerous thing you could attempt is a combination of all the various kinds of diving. Dress yourself up in full deep-sea diver's rig – you can get a huge brass helmet in most antique shops – and then arrange to have yourself hauled up into the air (a twin-engined helicopter might be safest). Then have the crew disconnect the cable and drop you a thousand feet onto a specially reinforced diving board, from which you will bounce into the air and then plummet beneath the waves, briefly waving at some clown fish, before you sink like a big fat stone to the ocean bed, where some coelacanths will stare at you as, still moving at some speed, you sink through the Earth's crust and are consumed by magma.

Or you could just go for a paddle.

TOMBSTONING

The clue is in the name. You would probably be better off jumping from an actual tombstone into a grave. The mistake most people make is thinking that jumping into the sea

The man who thought he was a lemming.

is a bit like doing a bomb at the swimming pool – but it's not. The sea is not a swimming pool; it is not a warm bath of widdle and chlorine whose surface is all churned up. It is a big flat sheet that, when you land on it, you go whack and break parts of you. The advantage of tombstoning is that you might impress a nine-year-old boy briefly; the disadvantage is that not only do you break your neck but you get wet as well.

SWIMMING THE CHANNEL

Formerly the preserve of men with stiff moustaches, swimming the Channel has got a bit common now and these days even television comedians can be seen doggy-paddling back and forth, spluttering a commentary to a film crew in a rowboat. It's actually dangerous for ferry companies to go to Boulogne and Dieppe now, so crowded is the sea with TV funnymen. Add to this the amount of people doing it for Comic Relief or just hoping to get a soggy autograph from a swimming stand-up, and it soon becomes clear that in the fairly near future the Channel will be so crammed with swimmers that although you may not actually be able to walk on their heads to France, you'll almost certainly be able to crowdsurf your way across.

So Channel swimming is no longer particularly dangerous.

Yes, we can see you!

If you really want to risk life and limb, we suggest that you try and swim the Channel Tunnel. It'll take ages and, if you're really lucky, you could get into the *Guinness Book of Records* as the first person to be run over by a train underwater.

SEA FISHING

Sea fishing is fairly dangerous, being essentially river fishing but on the end of a big jetty with waves crashing over it. And while you will, in your waders and big waterproof jacket, look more like a very fat woman pretending to be the French Lieutenant's Woman, there is a very real sense that you will be thrown into the sea by the sea itself. Not very contemplative, and an expensive form of risk taking as to be honest you might as well save all the money you'd spend on rods, lines, reels, and so forth, and just jump off a pier.

SEA FISHING ON A BOAT

Luxurious and only dangerous in very specific circumstances – when a giant shark leaps into the air and consumes you, head first. The chances of this happening ever are so slender that we do not recommend you bother.

TRAWLING

B.S. Johnson's excellent novel *Trawl* graphically describes life on a trawler – grim, cold, hard and, yes, Dangerous. Certainly it would be a soul-stiffening experience, but in the end the sheer volume of fish involved would get you down.

SHIPS

Ships are a very odd idea, being innately Dangerous. Most of us like being on land because the sea is a good place to get wet, get cold and get drowned. And yet for millions of years human beings have been hollowing out logs or gluing hides together or nailing planks into a pleasing shape just so they can Go To Sea. The idea of pushing yourself out onto the vasty deeps on top of some bits of wood is, frankly, ridiculous, but people seem to enjoy it. Have they not seen *The Perfect Storm* or read the Bible? The story of Noah's Ark alone would put any sane adult off seafaring, never mind Jonah and the Whale (which could equally well be titled Jonah and Some Very Nasty Sailors).

Here's a bit of word association. Say the word 'ship' to someone. Nine times out of ten they'll say 'wreck' (the other one time, the person thinks you said a rude word and walks off in a huff). There's a reason for this. Ships are about as safe as plugging a fork into a socket while lying in a bath full of piranha fish with swine flu.

So yes, if you want Danger, ships are the place to be, as this nautical Dangerous Guide shows.

PIRATES

One brilliantly Dangerous thing to do is to work on a cargo ship, either near Somalia or in the Gulf of Tonkin. This is because these places are crawling with actual pirates. Not the silly scarf-fondlers from *Pirates of the Caribbean*, but genuine evil, psychotic, unwashed, armed pirates. Imagine how good your slide show would be if halfway through working your passage to Taiwan you'd been hijacked by pirates and murdered! And also imagine how much better *Pirates of the Caribbean 3* would have been if they'd been captured by Somalis.

CRUISE SHIPS

Cruise ships used to be Dangerous, but this was because of a) icebergs and b) U-boats. These days the Germans are on our side and all the icebergs have melted. There is, however, one Dangerous thing you can do on a cruise – decide not to eat in your cabin. If you do this you will not only spend the next four weeks eating in the restaurant three times a day, but you will be eating WITH THE SAME PEOPLE. And given that these people are probably elderly rich people who spend their lives sailing around the world telling complete strangers about the cruises that they've been on, you will probably want to jump overboard round about Tuesday lunchtime ('I said to Abilene, aren't those the Johnsons? We met them in '98 on the sister ship to this very ship we're on now . . .')

Oh, and another common side effect of cruising is contracting the Norovirus, which may sound like the name of a ship ('Welcome aboard the SS *Norovirus*, sir!') but is in fact a hugely unpleasant vomiting bug. On board ship it's rather a waste of a disease, you might think, what with vomiting and the sea being closely connected, but there you go. Even more Dangerous.

'Call me Ishmael.'

LILOS

People have wasted thousands of hours searching for the perfect murder weapon. Generally it turns out to be a frozen leg of lamb, which for some reason the police investigating the murder eat while at the crime scene. Yes, because that's what murder investigators do, isn't it? Have a full Sunday roast while forensics dust around the sprouts. No, the ultimate murder weapon is the lilo. Simply persuade a rich elderly relative to sunbathe on one and push them out to sea. About three miles out the lilo will overturn and – hey presto! – you inherit a hundred pounds. Sea- or riverborn-lilos, used by oneself without a life jacket, are a form of aquatic Russian Roulette. Simply push yourself out into the Atlantic and enjoy the ride!

SUBMARINES

A lot safer than they were, except for Russian ones, which have a tendency to explode or sink, like bendy buses. Your best best for a bit of Dangerous fun is to somehow steal one of those one-man torpedos the Japanese used during World War 2. Either that or throw yourself off Beachy Head in a dustbin and hope for the best.

PADDLING

Always Dangerous these days with the hot weather. Jellyfish coming inland to see if anybody's left some crisps on the beach are a real risk. Rays can also lurk in six inches of water, although why they would want to do that is something of a mystery. And there's always the very real danger of accidentally standing at the exact spot where, five seconds from now, a sperm whale will decide to beach itself. THUD!

CHAPTER 20

DANGEROUS DRIVING

If one thing sums up a Middle-Aged Man doing his best in a Mid-Life Crisis – one thing, that is, apart from a beer belly and a sense of vague disillusion – it has to be the Dangerous Car. Even men who have never driven, men for whom the bus is the riskiest vehicle they've ever sat in, experience a visceral, primeval, post-watershed thrill when they think of Dangerous Cars. By which of course we don't mean some rusting piece of old toot that's only Dangerous because its coal-powered engine might explode in your face. Nor do we mean some vintage Trabant, always about to collapse like a soggy cardboard box on the motorway when you're trying to do 65 mph. No; we mean Dangerous Cars. Cars that are only made in red, or yellow. Cars whose engines sound like the death throes of a dragon that has worked all its life down an asbestos mine. Cars which can go from 0 to 60 in five seconds but nobody has ever driven them that slowly. Sports cars. Trophy cars. Muscle cars. Sex cars. You know, Dangerous Cars.

People look at Dangerous Cars and say that they are only bought by middle-aged men. That's because young men can't afford them – which is surely a good thing, because how many things do young men need anyway? They've already got the looks and the virility and the hair . . . surely they can leave something for the rest of us. Cowards flinch and traitors sneer and say that buying a Dangerous Car is just compensating for a small penis. So what? What are we supposed to buy? Giant penises? Hardly. Just as in life there are times to do the laundry and times to go into an Old People's Home, so there is a time in life to buy a Dangerous Car. And that time, if you are a Dangerous Middle-Aged Man, is now.

Really, when you think about it, there's nothing wrong here. The kids have left home (if they haven't, find a way to make sure they do, damn quick. You really don't want a bunch of teenagers anywhere near your car). Your wife will either be delighted with the new car, which means she's a total babe fox and the ideal partner for you in these, your difficult years, or she's a mardy fussbox, in which case she'd be better off with the dentist up the road, who she's been knocking off since 1998 and really ought to make an honest dentist of soon. Your bank manager will regard the new car as an act of folly and suggest that instead you use the money to bolster up your savings, shares and pensions; a perfect reminder to you that you still have some savings, shares and pensions which you can now cash in to pay for this car. Young women will be amused and horrified that a balding old geezer has got such a power-sex car; but when's the last time any young women were anywhere near enough to you to express even disapproval? You are three (or maybe four) steps away from LOTS OF FUN.

Make no mistake here, you are going to have fun. Even if you don't want to. The car, like some possessed '57 Plymouth in a Stephen King story, will siren-call to you at all hours. You'll be lying awake in bed, thinking about it. You'll be sneaking downstairs in your jim-jams to make sure it's all right. You'll be driving it at all hours. You'll be giving dolly birds lifts home at night from swanky nightclubs. You'll be taking out your mates from the pub. In short, you'll be exhausted. But it doesn't matter. You have a Dangerous Car, and you are King of the Road.

Porsche. Ferrari. MG. Why stop there? Richard Hammond drove a jet-powered car at 288 mph and he was a mere lad of 37. You're much older than him - get a real superfast test car, the kind you can normally only drive on some salt flats. Get a Batmobile (the old one that was sexy, not the one that looks like a tractor). Get a rocket-bike. The world, so long as you have got your seat belt on, is your oyster. And oysters - being seafood – are Dangerous, and sometimes they have pearls in them, which is plenty enough similes for our purposes.

Yes, there are downsides to owning a Dangerous Car. You may – quite literally – crash and burn. But look on the bright-side. James Dean was the king of '50s cool. He became even cooler when he crashed his Porsche Spider in 1955 at the age of 24. If you do the same thing, not only will you be as cool as James Dean *but you will have outlived him by several years.* See! It's good to be a Dangerous Middle-Aged Man!

Of course Dangerous Driving is frequently *less* about the vehicle you're driving and *more* about the conditions you're driving it in . . .

RAIN

Rain's pretty bad. Driving in the rain combines both slipperiness and wetness, neither of which make for good road-holding. Worse than that is ice, which is rain at its most devious and should be avoided. Then there's snow. Snow not only stops you driving but also keeps you trapped in your car until a St Bernard can be sent out. Oh, and then there's flooding, one of the more exciting side effects of rain, which also keeps you trapped in your car, but with very little chance of a St Bernard.

DESERTS

If there's no rain at all, of course, what you have is desert, which is rather bad for driving as well because of sand and heat and marauding tribes of Bedouin with quaint flintlocks. Deserts are thus Dangerous, but always seem to be part of a Round the World race, probably to add a bit of variety; also it's hard to go round a desert.

OFF-ROADING

To go off-roading, first you need an SUV. Amazingly, these cars were not actually designed to take children to school in North London but can actually be driven on rough terrain. So borrow one from a friend of the wife, and head for Danger, because the great thing about off-roading is that it's all risk. *On* the road is fairly straightforward because you will mostly encounter tarmac, with cars on it. *Off* the road is very Dangerous, because you don't know what the hell is going on. There could be rocks. There could be bogs. There could be pumas. Well, if a zoo has burned down. In any case, you take your life in your hands if you go off-roading.

To add spice to your off-roading, don't take that SUV. Go in a car that's manifestly unsuitable for your task. A Smart car, say, or a Morris Minor. That way you're bound to have an Adventure . . .

The North Yungas Road, feared and hated by drivers everywhere. A sort of Bolivian M25.

MOUNTAINS

Mountains are stupid places to drive, because not only do you keep having to change gear but one false move and you'll plummet thousands of feet to land in a small village, possibly killing a goat. This makes mountain driving Dangerous, which adds to the fun, especially if you don't like goats.

JEEPS AND LAND ROVERS

These things are ludicrously Dangerous. Jeeps are for a start really old, having been invented by Americans to look good in during World War Two. You wouldn't drive around now in an Austin from 1940, would you? And yet you think you're cool because you're jarring your coccyx every ten seconds in a bone-rattling Jeep. Land Rovers are the same, painful and uncomfortable and dangerous, so unpleasant in fact that the original marketing slogan for the Range Rover was rumoured to be: AT LAST – WE'VE MADE A CAR THAT WON'T CRIPPLE YOU.

QUAD BIKES

Specifically designed, it would seem, to injure people, quad bikes famously did as much harm to Ozzy Osbourne in ten seconds as forty years of drug and alcohol abuse. They look alluring, and fun, like go-karts for grown-ups, but in reality quad bikes are a kind of wheeled bucking bronco – after a brief moment of glory you are tossed into the air, from which you will fall to the ground and break everything inside you that can be broken.

MOTORBIKES

The official clichéd vehicle of Danger. People who ride motorbikes actually write clues to their state of mind on their jackets like LIVE FAST DIE YOUNG and I AM GOING TO DIE. Hell's Angels live each moment as if it were their last. And middle-aged men suddenly cash in their pensions and replace them with a brand new Harley-Davidson so they can look ridiculous on the M4 on a Sunday.

Motorbikes are genuinely dangerous because they crash into things and, less excitingly, you can fall off them. To fully appreciate the harm they can do, go to California where you

'Nigel! Sit up straight, dear!'

can ride a motorbike without a helmet. It's not known if Americans believe that wearing a 'doo rag' or cloth on your head is safer than wearing a helmet, but trust us, it doesn't work.

SCOOTERS

Some danger here of just being pulled off your vehicle and beaten to death – people who ride scooters are either wannabe Mods, who should know better and are really just playing dress-up, or total dickheads who work for advertising agencies and think riding a scooter is 'quirky'. Come on! If we all run together we can pull that chap off at the lights!

BICYCLES

Really dangerous. Even if you don't enter the Tour De France or some other horrific marathon which will wreck your health, just cycling around any British town is borderline fatal. For a start, everyone hates cyclists, believing them to be smug would-be eco warriors with the dress sense of a Belgian disco star. They're also extremely vulnerable, as they don't wear any clothes. Also they have the annoying habit of a) cycling on the pavement, where they are sure to get clobbered and b) telling pedestrians to 'get out of the road', which will make it even surer that they will get clobbered.

BICYCLE TUK-TUKS

A Dangerous way of making a few bob. With a tuk-tuk – which is one of those motorised tricycles with a big back seat for tourists to sit in – you are at the mercy of a double edged sword. Not only are drunks liable to attack you late at night, but all black-cab drivers loathe tuk-tuks and will go out of their way to run them down. Risky!

CHAPTER 21

HAZARDOUS COMPUTERS

We believe it was the fine comedian Richard Herring who redefined the word 'history' as: 'what you clear on your computer when your wife is coming into the room.' And although clearly you are not that sort of person, that statement does illustrate one of the great truths of life – computers are extremely Dangerous. You only have to look at the movies, which are the repositories of all great truths. On telly, in science fiction and that, computers are our friends, advising us on how best to defeat the enemy and often teaching us maths using brightly coloured images of fruit. But this is all deception. Computers want us to be their friend. Computers want us to sit back and let them tell us what to do. But that's telly. In the movies, things are more sinister. All computers are bad. So bad that they make robots look good. Because there are always good robots or, if they're Arnold Schwarzenegger, robots who have been bad and are now good (and sometimes robots who were bad, went good and are now bad again. It's all rather confusing).

But movie computers are never good, except for that slightly wet one in *Electric Dreams*. Look at HAL in 2001, lip-reading and giving interviews and lying and singing music-hall songs. Look at the one in *Demon Seed*, whose not unreasonable wish is to make love to Julie Christie but who goes about it in the most caddish manner. Look at the lady computer in *I, Robot*, who not only wants to make humanity do her bidding, but follows Will Smith around everywhere telling him off. And look at the bad computer in the film *Wall-E*, whose aim is to prevent the human race returning to Earth.

And this is just the fictional background world of computers. Because ever since Alan Turing tricked some computers into helping him decode some German, mankind has played dice with computers, a lot, and not done very well. So be warned: when you play with computers, you play with fire.

PRESSING BUTTONS

The most Dangerous thing you can do with a computer is turn it on. The second-most Dangerous thing you can do is press any buttons. Computer manufacturers know this; how many times have you opened a program or started a game or anything and been greeted with – not, as is sensible, BE REALLY CAREFUL: THIS COMPUTER IS MENTAL but PRESS ANY KEY. Those three words make as much sense as writing PUT THIS IN YOUR MOUTH on a machine gun.

And the simile extends, because what is using a computer but a modern form of Russian Roulette? Admittedly, you'd have to actually work at the Pentagon to destroy the world with a computer but even at home you can do a fair old bit of damage with a common or garden laptop. There are buttons on the average PC which look innocuous but, once pressed, will send your accounts to hell. Even the

Scan Result: Virus *W32.Sircam.Worm@mm* found. File NOT
cleaned.

This file contains a computer worm, a program that spreads
very quickly over the Internet to many computers and can
delete files, steal sensitive information, or render your machine
unusable.

This attachment has a virus that may infect your computer.
It cannot be cleaned.
We recommend that you DO NOT download this
attachment.

Goodbye, Tuesday!

whiter-than-white Mac can, at the tap of a key, send your
precious wedding-video files – which you promised your wife
you'd finally get put onto DVD – into a kind of trash bin from
which there is literally no ESC.

So have fun playing Robot Roulette with your computer
– write your whistleblowing exposé of your former employer
on a computer and then, instead of copying it, onto a hard
drive or whatever it is people do, just close your eyes and stab
at the keyboard with one finger. Where will the file go? Into
the history books or into the ether? It's all very exciting.

And to make it even more exciting, and Dangerous, why
not introduce a child into the equation? You've almost
certainly got a child knocking around somewhere, doing
nothing useful and eating your food and watching your telly,
so put it to good use. After all, if they could climb chimneys
and operate looms back in the old days, chances are that they
might still have other residual skills that could be of use
to you. Right now all you need to do is find a child with no
abilities at all. This is an advanced form of Computer
Roulette. If a child presses the keys of a piano at random, the

worst that can happen is an inoffensive, tuneless noise. If the same child randomly presses the keys on your computers, you can literally spend years trying to retrieve the loss.

HACKING

Fun and profit! Most hackers seem to be motivated entirely by showing off – hacking into the Pentagon's war computer, for example – which just goes to show that this sort of thing ought to be left to those best suited to it, i.e. the Dangerous Man. For you are no callow youth of 19, trying to impress some other nerds with your knowledge of Basic or Lantana 547. You are a grown-up who wants to buy an Aston Martin with which to impress 19-year-old girls. You have some understanding of how the world works. And you have borrowed your son's PC. So get cracking and get hacking – why not break into the Ministry of Defence's computer system? It can't be that hard – most of their employees seem to leave their laptops on the train or in the backs of taxis. Why not go into the database for MPs' expenses and add a couple of zeroes? Or hack into the *Heat* magazine editorial files and insert a load of libellous stories about celebs? Then call up all these people and ask for a million quid in used tenners to be deposited in a sack at a location of your choosing. They'll pay up. Oh yes. Or, possibly, have a sniper shoot you when you turn up. It's a risk, but isn't that what this book is all about?

SURFING THE NET

This is always fun. Just putting random words into a search engine can lead you, like an innocent in a red-light district, to some extraordinary places. Even the most innocuous word, like 'furniture' or 'scat', has meanings on the wobbly World Wide Web that have occurred to very few of us. With this in mind, open a dictionary at random, stab in a few words on Google, and then do exactly what the website you've staggered into tells you to. Ecstasy may await. Jail may beckon. Either way, you're no longer bored and you haven't even had to leave the room, never mind the house.

EGO SURFING

One of the great modern Dangers. Sort of the opposite of the experience of the protagonist in Bread's terrifically sad and ironic song 'Diary'. He found a diary under a tree and it was full of lovely, lovelorn words about him – but on reading on he learned she loved not him but another! Well, ego surfing's a sinister cousin of that, really – you put your name in a computer and you discover that, to paraphrase writer and broadcaster Armando Iannucci, you have walked into a room where everyone is throwing human waste at you (and this is a man who's fairly popular). Had the protagonist in *Bread*'s diary looked himself up online he would have found that everything was about him, and it was really, really unpleasant.

A simple search for (say) the author of *The Dangerous Book For Middle-Aged Men* – the sort where, y'know, one isn't really looking for praise, oh no, just a few words of neutral acknowledgement and, well, maybe, some praise would be nice – within nanoseconds turns into a horrific post-libellous bloodbath of personal remarks, uncontrolled invective and just generally spectacular nastiness.

It's clearly not worth it. However, if you fancy a bit of Danger in your life, then this is the place to go. Like taking a cold shower only with frozen nails instead of water, ego surfing is more bracing than a kind of cyborg Skegness that's out to get you. As Nietzsche said when *Man And Superman* got a massive slagging in *Sounds*, what does not destroy us makes us incredibly angry. And that's always a fun place to be.

PCs AND MACs

The world is divided into two kinds of people, MacUsers and people who own PCs. As a statement, of course, that's deeply flawed. It's a bit like saying the world is divided into two kinds of people, members of the House of Castile and Aragon and people who aren't members of the House of Castile and Aragon. Because while the Apple Corporation seem to be awful popular vis-à-vis telephones and mp3 players, they don't – comparatively speaking – shift that many computers when set alongside PCs. Perhaps this is because PCs are sold in a shop called a World whereas Macs are sold in sort of shelters in alleyways by old Japanese guys with weird eyepieces like in that film *Blade Runner*. PCs therefore are risky things to own because they are dead common. You'll never impress a woman by claiming to own a PC. Then again, you'll never impress a woman by claiming to own any kind of computer, or anything to do with computers. Women just don't care. However, you will never impress anyone by claiming to own a Mac – except a nerd. And if you really want to take your life in hand and use it to beat the hell out of your soul, then do something which allies you with a nerd.

Computers are nerdy enough as it is without buying the nerd's own computer, which is what an Apple Mac is. Never mind the clean design and easy functionality, buying a Mac is the equivalent of owning a life-size-model light sabre, or a working Dalek.

If your idea of a risk is being mistaken for a nerd when really you're deeply cool, then flirt with danger and buy a Mac. Everyone else in the world just buys a PC and doesn't tell anyone.

VIRUSES

Surely the most exciting – and therefore Dangerous – thing about computers. Viruses – classic overexcited computer word there – are a bit like real viruses in that they spread and reproduce. But then, lots of other, less frightening things spread and reproduce, like hamsters and moss. We can only suppose that people would be unable to sell security software by saying THIS SOFTWARE PROTECTS AGAINST HAM-STERS. The fact is that computer viruses are called viruses to make them look more frightening, like those flies which pretend to be wasps. Most computer viruses are far from harmful. Oh no! This virus has sent itself to every address in your address book! Goodness! Help! This virus has prevented you from playing *Frogger* on the bus! Run away!

Yes, there are computer viruses which can do lots of harm to your PC (even viruses can't be bothered with Macs) but it's hardly Armageddon, is it? If all the bubonic plague and Spanish flu had been able to do was stop your adding machine or abacus from working, we wouldn't be talking about them now, would we? But they killed people, not Nintendogs online, so calm down everybody.

Nevertheless, if you want to be slightly Dangerous send out one of those hysterical virus-related emails. You know the kind of thing:

'WARNING! If you receive an email from "JIB JOBS" or "THIS IS YOUR MUM", delete it IMMEDIATELY! It contains the Ring Modulator Virus which will not only spread around the world and destroy every computer on earth but also gives you scratchy skin. It is UNSTOPPABLE. Unless you delete it, which is a bit stoppable when you think about it.'

But leave out the last sentence.

COMPUTER GAMES

Computer games are largely rubbish. There is a clue in the name: 'games.' Not games of skill and the mind like chess and that, but games like shooting and driving a pretend car. In the real world these are called Cowboys And Indians and Mister Brrum Brrum. Other computer games are equally feeble, involving as they do little men running around grabbing cabbages. The whole thing is pretty grim and even those more stimulating programs where you create your own city or run a family are little more than the creepy side of being on your local council. The only danger here, as with so many things, is that your brain decides to kill itself before it turns into three pints of neural slop.

The only games that do present an opportunity for actual Danger are those ones which use your own real-world physicality and force the player to actually stand up and throw themselves about the room. Called, with shocking disregard for double entendre, Wii games, these games are engaging because while they may dispense with boxing gloves and tennis racquets and golf clubs and so on, they also offer the very real chance that you may hurt yourself, something previously only possible with real games like rugby and hockey.

So have Dangerous fun with your Wii games. And why not add a frisson of extra Danger by incorporating the Wii handset into an actual baseball bat, pair of boxing gloves or fencing sword? That way you should be able to take a few people with you as well as knocking out your own teeth. Now that's a proper game!

ONLINE GAMBLING

In real life, gambling is tricky. Apart from horses, which is easy. What we mean is the kind where you have to dress as James Bond and go into a special building and drink things and know about cards and dice. Not the sort of thing you can exactly pop out for ten minutes and do:

PARTNER: Where are you going?
YOU: Um. To the gym.
PARTNER: In a dinner jacket?
YOU: It's a very expensive gym.

Unlikely. Whereas on the internet, computer gambling is a piece of cake. There is nobody there to warn you off, no sudden glances into an empty wallet or crowds of beautiful women and monocled Frenchmen to glumly wander off as soon as it becomes apparent that you are a rotten gambler. It's just you and your credit card, at four a.m., on the laptop, getting increasingly desperate, increasingly broke and, worst of all, as you get worse and broker, increasingly optimistic.

Watch your soul cry as you move from poker to backgammon to roulette, each new game indicating not that you are a kind of gambling renaissance man but rather that you are universally bad at 'trying your luck.' See your common sense leave with an angry slam of your brain door as you email your virtual bank for more real funds. And listen to your bowels work their way through all the elements as you lose in this order your mind, your house, and your family.

On the other hand, you might WIN!

EBAY

The most Dangerous place on the internet. eBay, as it thinks it's written, thereby destroying five hundred years of cogent spelling at a keystroke, is in many ways worse than gambling online, because at least with gambling there's a faint chance that you might win something unexpected and brilliant like Italy or a banjo. Whereas with eBay, all you will 'win' is what you were looking for in the first place, and the only surprise will be how much you have agreed to pay for it. And 'win' is the word they use here, hinting at a sense of victory that really ought to be absent upon the purchase of a complete set of *Star Trek: The Next Generation* shot glasses.

It's not winning, is it? It's shopping. If you are at the till in Sainsbury's the cashier doesn't ask you what you're planning to 'win' in your shopping trolley. She just asks you for money. You don't go into the pub with the vague hope of 'winning' a pint of beer. Imagine how that would pan out. Every couple of days the landlord shows his customers a photograph of a pint of beer and invites them to bid for it. There'd be chaos. You wouldn't stand for it. And yet that's what you do on eBay, and not even for a pint of beer. Still, it's a gamble and gambling can be fun!

The cliché of eBay is of course that everyone does it when they're drunk and then regrets it the next day. This makes eBay sound like sex, except you can do eBay all night and generally you don't have to sign for a baby. In fact, eBay lacks even the brief triumphal moment of sex, because it goes from anticipation to depression without the climax in between, no matter how much you may punch the air in unconvincing triumph.

Making eBay Dangerous is not particularly difficult, given that it's already pretty risky. There's the risk to your relationship – partners are rarely pleased to find that you've stayed up all night on the internet, and even less so when they learn that you've forgone a night with them not even for virtual sex with a famous naughty lady but for a collection of limited-edition James Bond pocket watches that were somehow cheap because you bid more than anyone else for them – a rationale which makes no sense to anyone but you. There's the risk to your wallet – again, it is not saving money to buy something, but spending it. And there's the risk to your sanity, when you cannot actually remember why you thought a series of realistic figurines of members of Echo and the Bunnymen was something you really needed.

The most Dangerous fun you can have with eBay is to reverse the usual process; instead of putting in a low bid and hoping it's accepted, follow the bidding until the minute before the last minute and then put in a huge ridiculous bid. If you lose, it's because someone has been tricked, by you, into making an even more hugely ridiculous bid. If you win, you're stuffed, but hey, that's eBay.

VERY RUDE SITES

Oh dear. You don't need us to tell you that it's inadvisable to look at these things. But should you be tempted, please be aware that you're always only one click way from something truly, spectacularly appalling. There are Dangers even a Dangerous Man should avoid. Unless you really can't think of another way to spend the rest of your life in a jail for perverts.

Oh, and if you do avoid jail, then also be careful to avoid spending any money. Not only will your true love see your credit-card bill – which will appear to have all the things like 'spanners' and 'family holiday' on it in tiny letters and PORN!!!! DIRTY PORN!!!! in huge neon script – but also for the rest of your life you will receive the most appalling spam which, rightly or wrongly, assumes you are a sex-crazed pervert with a very small penis. And nobody wants to be called that.

DOWNLOADS

Downloads, if you've been away, are those things that you can get off the internet which used to come on shiny silver discs – songs, movies, TV shows, games, that sort of thing. And they are very Dangerous, for several reasons. One is that official downloads are quite expensive and why would you want a tiny version of a DVD or a song or a game when you can have a full-sized one, in a box, that you don't have to watch on a computer? That's not particularly Dangerous but it is annoying, which could lead to apoplexy, whatever that is. More Dangerous is the fact that you have illegal downloads. These can contain viruses, which as we've seen isn't that dangerous but is rather annoying if you've just downloaded series eighteen of *The Wire*, the one where everyone gets shot, and it's just pixels and your iPod throws up. Worse, they are often not what they seem to be and your cool advance bootleg release of *Public Enemies II* will turn out to be some madness called *Obama's Secret Lies* and mad people will email you and try to get you to join the Illuminati or something absurd like that.

Oh, and the really dangerous thing about illegal downloads is that they're illegal and you can be prosecuted. And while this is true, it's only actually worrying if you're a fifteen-year-old girl living in Florida; the rest of us are perfectly safe. So go on! Destroy the entertainment industry!

WIKIPEDIA

Like a politician, Wikipedia is only dangerous if you believe it. This is partly because the world's largest organic encyclopedia is written by amateurs – and don't write in, we mean 'amateurs' in the way that gentlemen cricketers and the like were once described as amateurs i.e. they were very good and didn't get paid for it – happy now? Amateurs who have a wide knowledge of their chosen subject, so wide in fact that sometimes whilst trying to ford their subject they get lost, wade about for a while and drown. But it's also partly because nutcases also write Wikipedia – and again, don't write in: by 'nutters' we don't mean violent people, just people who should be locked up for being mental. These are the ones who erase ten pages of accurate information about, say, Abba, and replace them with the words ABBA ARE THE BEST BAND IN THE WORLD AND I HOPE YOU GET A DISEASE IF YOU DISAGREE WITH ME. While undoubtedly true, and heartfelt, this is not information you can really use.

Most troubling about Wikipedia, of course, are the outright lies that people insert. A perfectly reasonable piece about, for example, Spenser Perceval, who is, astonishingly, the only British Prime Minister ever to have been assassinated (like, think of the candidates!), might begin with a few dates and career milestones, and then go on like this: 'Perceval was the instigator of the window tax. He did this because he wanted to marry Lord Nelson and clean his windows.' You see? It might be true. It isn't but it might be. And one day you could find yourself quoting that in a pub full of pretty girl historians whom you had hoped to impress. Again, not terrifically likely, but you never know.

So turn this problematic aspect to your advantage. Subvert Wikipedia to your own ends. Sign in before an important meeting and change important facts that might be useful to your opponent. When he says, say, 'We should invest in solar power' butt in and say, 'But solar power gives smallpox to little boys and girls', and when he protests show everyone the Wikipedia page. The danger is, of course, that somebody might have some real information about their person, but the times being what they are, frankly, you could show them some information you'd got from *Heat* magazine and they'd believe you.

INTERNET DATING

Another highly dangerous activity. Computer, or internet, dating is very much a risky business. It's not that far away from *Second Life*, in fact, in that the face you put on is, inevitably, not the real you. And while you're unlikely to go on an internet dating site and claim to be Valianticon, the winged knight of the Ruby Mountains, you are equally unlikely to tell anything remotely like the truth about yourself. The internet doesn't play like that; it makes you a liar. So right there, opportunities for Danger. Because even if you do, by some astonishing fluke, tell the truth about yourself – MIDDLE-AGED MAN, DRESSED BADLY, FORMERLY GSOH ERODED BY LIFE, WANTS TO MEET ASTONISHINGLY GOOD-LOOKING PERSON FOR SEX AND MAYBE A RELATIONSHIP BUT PROBABLY JUST SEX – the chances are extremely high that the person replying will be a dirty great big liar.

So there's that: when you enter into an internet date, you are essentially going along with a box of lies and a bouquet of falsehoods. And that's if it goes well; at least when NON-SMOKER, 28ISH, PETITE turns out to be CHAIN-SMOKER, 43 IF SHE'S A DAY, ENORMOUS, you know where you are. Maybe love will form between you; after all, she's also thinking that you are no oil painting. But the problem is this: you don't know what else is going on here; there may be more to this than meets the eye. Which is always the case with internet dating; as with everything else in life, there's a high chance that everybody else apart from you is insane, or Dangerous, or both.

Still, lying is a Dangerous game these days, because you can't just say, 'Yes, I'm a test pilot, ooh, very Dangerous, mm, planes' because as soon as you've gone for a jimmy riddle your date will be on her mobile phone looking you up on Google. And then you're done for. So you need to construct an identity. Set up your own website and call it retiredtestpilot.com. Hack into Wikipedia and give yourself your own page. Or, as if we're honest this is less time-consuming, just become a test pilot. Because unfortunately with the net, the truth is out there, and if you tell lies people have revenge strategies. They can put photos of you up on the web. They can have strangers mark you from 1 to 10 for ugliness, dress sense or just general looking-duffness.

Go for it if you must. The thrill of deception is never keener than when internet dating. But beware – there is always the terrible risk of being Babooshka'd. Named after the Kate Bush song, this ploy relates to the age-old problem of posing as a younger, sexier version of yourself on a date – only to find that you have in fact arranged to go out with your own partner, who is also posing as a younger version of herself. This is extremely confusing as she is cheating with someone who isn't you, while you are cheating with someone who isn't her, but in fact neither of you are cheating, which is rather dull. Online this can go even more wrong, as one day you arrive at a restaurant and discover that, somehow, you have gone on a date with yourself. Enjoy!

SOCIAL NETWORKING

The Danger here is that you might waste your life, like that man in the *Twilight Zone* who thought that as everyone else had died he had loads of time to read books and then he broke his glasses. Of course, these days he could have printed the books out in large print or just got some reading specs in Boots, but there are contemporary modern dangers out there, and they are all on social networking sites. Twitter, Facebook, Plaxo – they always sound like the sort of person who would be an enemy of Superman in one of his more novelty phases, and they are certainly just as irritating and silly.

But they are also fatal. Apart from the fact that you get NO WORK DONE and so are useful only if you want to get sacked, they are also bad because they take up all of your time, and one day you will turn on your computer to find these messages from your children and partner:

@smithfamily: we are off. Your dinner's not in the oven because the oven's in the charity shop.

It's one way of getting a divorce, we suppose. But there are more fun Dangerous things out there.

UNRELIABLE AVATARS

Once upon a time an avatar was a thing in Hindu mythology, the incarnation of a higher being. It isn't now. An avatar nowadays is your online representative, a version of you that you design and control and use to wander about in cyberspace, in programs like *Second Life*. You don't have to actually be a Hindu god any more, you can just do yourself up as one.

'Hang on! This isn't Planet Sex!'

163

The main connection between avatars of yore and the now kind of avatar is that avatars still look very groovy – immense Grecian heroes or heroines striding around with frankly rather full chests, looking all chiselled as they thrust about the place with their oddly enormous buttocks bobbing about like displaced Belisha beacons on top of thighs like Nelson's Column and doing all sorts of godly things. Like flying, or leaping from tall buildings, or smiting people, or just sitting on their columnar haunches and lookin' good. Yes, it's great to be an avatar.

Of course, as we all know, in real life people resemble their avatars not one jot. The great cliché of the internet is that the cooler your avatar, the uncooler you yourself are. Just as driving a sports car traditionally indicated a tidgy winkle, so having an avatar called Pangeon the Munificator with huge wings and muscles like a walnut orgy strongly suggests that you yourself are a morbidly obese man in sweat pants and a Powderpuff Girls T-shirt who lives with your mum. In a world where all the gods are vanquished, basically, it is the nerds that rule. (For some reason, nobody has gone the other way. It is extremely doubtful that Governor Schwarzenegger of California, for example, stuffs his bulk behind a tiny B&Q workstation and goes into *Second Life* with an avatar called Vern who has skinny little arms and wears glasses from Boots.)

What has this got to do with the Dangerous Man? You're not a nerd, well, not any more. You're Dangerous! The answer is this: there are certain advantages to having an avatar. You can escape the daily grind without actually being able to fly, or leap tall buildings. You can also escape other niggles, like being a bit bald in real life, or not having been to the gym much. And you can go anywhere and do anything. Free your mind, as the song nearly goes, and your avatar will follow. The people you meet in cyberspace don't need to know that you're only cruising around *Second Life* while your wife is taking the library books back, or that your avatar is called Kalgon because that was the first name you saw on a box of limescale remover you had spilled and were vacuuming up before your wife got home from the library.

Here you can be a god. Here none challenge your word. And here you might meet a goddess. Although – and this does seem obvious, but even in cyberspace love is blind – the goddess you meet, She-Love of Sexnowvia, is almost certainly not a seven-foot-tall Amazon skilled in the arts of love and war. She's probably a trucker from Rhyl called Marjorie who's getting over a messy divorce.

Tread carefully, then. In fact, tread very carefully. There have been *Second Life* actions with consequences in First, or real, Life. In 2008, a British couple who met in a web chat room and got married both on the internet and in a registry office in Saint Austell divorced after the wife caught the husband 'having sex with a virtual prostitute'. The phrase 'virtual prostitute' doesn't mean, as you might think, someone who appears on *Big Brother* and *I'm A Celebrity*, but is in fact some sort of horrible cyber transaction that perhaps we shouldn't dwell on for too long.

And isn't this *Second Life* thing a bit childish? Like learning Klingon or collecting *Star Wars* toys, living in *Second Life* is a slightly retarded variant on the dressing-up box. We all like a fancy-dress party, but all the time? It's like being one of those slightly mentally unadept people who have Christmas dinner every day. It's not right. Maybe if you are going to enter the world of cyberspace you should keep the whole avatar thing but stay away from the pseudoporn kindergarten of *Second Life*. It's certainly useful and fun to have a godlike representative in cyberspace, but why not use it to pop into your cyberbank and have a word in person about your over-draft, possibly hanging your cyberbank manager out of a cyber window? And maybe you could use your avatar to take back all the things you bought on eBay when you were drunk that time? Go on, live Dangerously.

CHAPTER 22

FOOD DANGEROUS FOOD (& DRINK)

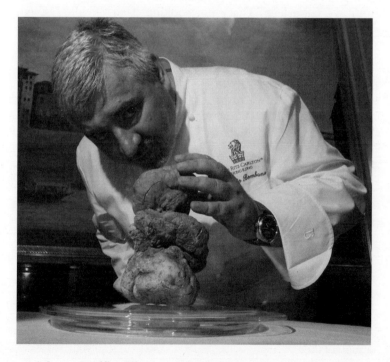

A huge truffle. The pig who found it is still telling his mates, 'It was this big, honest.'

ooking is a subject to be approached with caution. For the Dangerous Man, it is not simply a business of making some food hot and then eating it. That's what your mum does. There's a lot more to it than that for the Dangerous Man. For him, cooking is a test of endurance, knowledge and, if we're honest, showing off.

Normal cooking goes like this. Mum (or wife, or son, or *au pair* you have somehow married) goes to supermarket, buys basic ingredients – chicken, mushrooms, milk, spuds – and makes the dinner. Everyone eats the dinner, rubs their stomachs and says, 'That was great, mum, now let's watch television until we fall asleep.' That's not cooking. That's feeding. Even sparrows can feed other sparrows, and sometimes a cuckoo.

Dangerous Cooking is very different. For a start, it doesn't involve 'buying stuff'. It requires 'sourcing ingredients'. They may sound like the same thing, only one is a bit more Latiny, but they're not. Buying ingredients is a piece of, as it were, cake. That's what supermarkets are for. They have actual shelves, actually labelled, with the names of stuff. Most of the stuff is in tins. Some of the stuff is peeled, or washed, or even cooked. It's not very Dangerous.

Dangerous Cooking begins, then, with Dangerous Shopping. Except it doesn't. It begins, like all great expeditions, with preparation. Your Dangerous Cook spends hours planning the dish he is going to make. And like Scott going to the Antarctic or Drake off to the New World, he makes a list of things he will need, esoteric and special things about which a normal person would say things like, 'You don't need that, it's the same as normal milk' or 'What the bloody hell is a matsutake?'

The shopping list, as it will be called once it's been formulated, is a cross between a busy morning for Heston Blumenthal and *The Chronicles Of Narnia*. It will be exotic, confusing, and partly fictional. It will contain things that you couldn't actually get in Britain before 1998, and it will feature some things that may have gone extinct since the recipe was written ('Take sixteen dodos . . .'). It would baffle a spotty lad at Lidl. It would induce head-scratching in a manager at Waitrose. And, quite frankly, even a Frenchman might find it a touch poncey.

Stage two is shopping. Again, this cannot be done in the local supermarket. The corner shop's out, although some obscure Indian spices may be sourceable here. It has to be that beacon for the middle-aged man in search of adventure, the Farmers' Market.

Farmers' Markets aren't places where farmers do their shopping – they go to Tesco like the rest of us – but markets where, as the name suggests, farmers flog all the stuff that the EU doesn't want to buy up and burn. And, as they are competing with real shops where you can get normal food very cheaply, farmers' markets have to sell – Dangerous Food. Food that costs a lot of money. Food that your nan wouldn't like. Food whose name rolls off the tongue and that's about it, fun for the tongue-wise. Sprouting broccoli – for people who need more than one kind of broccoli as opposed to, like most of us, people who don't need any kind of broccoli. Shitake mushrooms, for people who like their mushrooms to taste of soap. And truffles. Nobody really knows what truffles are but we all know two things about them. They grow at the base of trees and pigs can find them. Neither of these things sounds like a recommendation but the genius thing – the Dangerous thing about them is that truffles are really, really expensive. They don't taste of soap. They taste of HOW MUCH??!!!!!

The Dangerous Man, moving through the Farmers' Market like Indiana Jones through a bazaar, his little wire basket banging against his hip like a Luger, is alert to the dangers of the market. Farmers selling things too cheaply. Red-cheeked farmers' wives offering things he can get in Asda. Cakes and pies. Nice food. The Dangerous Man avoids all temptations and buys the sprouting broccoli, the shitake mushrooms, the Normandy pear brandy and, of course, the truffles.

Once home and safe, his wallet empty and weeping, the Dangerous Man has his greatest challenge – he has to actually cook all this stuff. This sounds like a chore but it's not. Because the Dangerous Man has invested the money he was putting aside for his pension in state-of-the-art kitchenware. He's got those Japanese knives that can behead a fish just by being in the same room. He's got Le Creuset pans and griddles. He's got a steamer from the Chinese shop that's just like the one in *Kung Fu Panda*, so it's ironic as well as useful. And he's got a George Foreman grill, to do the actual cooking with, because his ex-wife hid the instruction book with the new Freon cooker when she found out he'd spent her as well as his own pension on knives.

The meal, let us assume, turns out badly. This is part of the frisson, the Danger. Will it be edible? Will it be actually toxic? There's only one way of finding out. Get some friends around, dosh them out a load of Normandaise pear brandy so they can't feel their taste buds, and impress them so much with your presentation – lots of nice plates and those forks that fall over on their side 'cos their handles are shaped like Toblerones – that they won't notice they're mostly eating fungus.

Why not just have some nice fish fingers?

CONSUME WITH CARE: EDIBLES

Blowfish – or 'fugu' – are the world's number one danger food. The poison of the blowfish, which is contained in its liver, muscles, ovaries and skin, is 1,200 times more potent than cyanide, but probably not as nice (cyanide is almondy, like a tagine). And as everyone knows, the Japanese like nothing more than to cook a poisonous fish and charge a lot of money for it. In the West, where you can get food poisoning much more cheaply, we don't do that sort of thing. There's really no need to, either: why spend a fortune on agonising pain and death when you can just eat some undercooked chicken – for best results we recommend you get your four-year-old child to defrost and barbecue the chicken for you.

If you are tired of our bland British diet, there's really no need to look to Japan for your Dangerous dining opportunities. Not when there are so many other exciting options. Christmas, for example, is famous for both lots of food and lots of unpleasant social interaction. But, given that holly – berries cause nausea, vomiting and diarrhoea – and mistletoe – arrows made from it kill Norse gods – are both pretty poisonous, how about garnishing a few meals with the odd sprig? It might involve a trip to casualty on Christmas Day but it beats watching the actual Christmas Day edition of *Casualty*.

And if you're the adventurous type and are prepared to travel, there is one dish you simply must try. From New Guinea, we present, and would deign to introduce to the world's gastronomic table, the world's only poisonous bird – the pitohui. The pitohui have poisonous skin and feathers, and for some weird reason exude the same toxin as poisonous frogs, which is taking admiration a step further than usual. The best of the pitohuis is the hooded pitohui, which is distinguishable by its crest and the fact that it absolutely stinks. Natives call the hooded pitohui the 'rubbish bird', which is a bit harsh, but you can see where they're coming from.

Should you be unable to visit New Guinea to excite your taste buds, there is a cheaper alternative. Eat a butterfly. The Monarch butterfly, which is attractive but in a sort of tacky way, like it was bought in Argos, begins its life as a caterpillar which loves to eat milkweed. Milkweed is a poisonous plant, and so if you're a bird that eats a Monarch butterfly, you'll be sick (it is not known what would happen if you fed a Monarch to a pitohui). But beware, Danger fans, there is a

*Once a year, Monarch butterflies swarm
on Alan Bennett.*

non-poisonous butterfly called the Viceroy, which mimics the
Monarch's colouring to avoid being eaten. So whatever you
do, butterfly gastronomes, don't try and buy a Viceroy on
eBay unless it comes with some sort of butterfly certificate.

How about some cheese? The Italian cheese Casu Marzu
is a delightful pecorino cheese which is fermented by
maggots and banned by the EU. The locals say it's safe to eat
if it's crawling with maggots, and if not then it's best to leave
it alone. Failing that, there are loads of things you can eat
that are very bad for you indeed. Mushrooms, of course. If
anyone offers you a Death Cap, a Destroying Angel, or a

Deadly Webcap, be careful. As their names gently hint these mushrooms are very toxic, so only eat them if you think you're too fat, or too alive. Other things you can eat to spice up what may no longer be your life include rhubarb, chocolate and old spuds – although you'd have to eat enormous amounts of these foods to get ill. Scientists we asked estimated that you'd need to consume ten times your body weight, or twenty times if you're only little. But hey! Isn't that what people do now? One of the great advantages of modern life is that, now morbid obesity is the norm, you have carte blanche to eat as much rhubarb, chocolate and old spuds as you like!

And, apparently, tapioca, although you really would have to be suicidal if you felt drawn to that vile mess of plant-spawn.

DO NOT TAKE ORALLY: INEDIBLES

People have long ago moved away from the outdated concept of only eating things that are actually food. *The Guiness Book of Records* is a veritable junkyard of record-breaking attempts to eat razor blades, swords, coins and other metal items. And you don't even have to want to be a record-breaker. Just start small, with something harmless like leaves, and work your way up. If you've ever wanted to find out what happens to bone china inside the human digestive system, then there really is one simple way to find out. And how about the world of metaphors? Mix oil and water and drink that. Or enjoy a picnic with some chalk and cheese. The world, if not your dinner, is your oyster.

'Hmm, the taste is rather sharp.'

THE DANGERS OF DRINK

All drinking is dangerous if it's done properly. Absinthe makes the heart go mental, for example, but even beer and wine can do the trick. The best Dangerous thing about alcohol is that it creeps up on one; you can drink a bottle of whisky every day and you might not die before five or six days have passed. And the great thing about alcohol is that it's a fun way to go. Drinking arsenic is just boring, frankly, while history does not record that when Socrates drank hemlock he then went out and knocked a policeman's helmet off before dying.

The strongest drink in the world is supposed to be Everclear Grain Alcohol which is 95 per cent proof. It is also entirely flavourless, unless being completely pissed is a flavour. You may prefer the aniseedy madness of absinthe, though, which can make you hallucinate, and is a drink so scary that America banned it for eighty years. Both these drinks are very Dangerous, but they are limited in their effects by the fact that they're designed to make you happy. To really experience a Dangerous Drink, try energy drinks. These ludicrous concoctions give you 'energy' by dosing you up with epic quantities of caffeine and sugar. You would be just as well off eating granules of Nescafé from the jar.

(HAPTER 23

UNSUITABLE PETS

Pep up your daily existence by having something genuinely life-threatening under your own roof. This is easier than it sounds. For most of your life, if you've been a sensible man, you've probably had a pet timeline like this:

AGE 0–5: fake pet. These are the years of the pretend animal, the teddy bear, the stuffed lion and the chewed boa constrictor. For many men, it is as near as they will ever get to real bears, lions and snakes.

AGE 5–10: miniature pet. This is the Time of the Rodent, when boys are allowed at best a large hamster or a pensive gerbil, and at worst some sort of mouse or shrew. The child with really meek parents may end up even worse off, with a stick insect or a caterpillar. Mouse or insect, any pet that can be eaten by another pet is no damn good.

AGE 10–40: dog.

And that's it. For a huge part of a man's life, the pet that life has allocated him will be a dog (if you want a cat, clearly you should move to Paris and start painting big women). Dogs are great, but they do vary. Although if you have a partner, and you have children, the dogs you are permitted to own will not vary much at all. They will be drawn from the spaniel, or toy, range of dogs. Toy dogs are aptly named because they are small, children love them and if you break them it's easier to buy a new one than get it mended. Spaniel dogs are deceptive; they often advertise themselves as romping things, ready to snatch a trout from the stream or bring down a pheasant from the air, but when you get one home you find it just lies on its fluffy hocks and eats chocolate from the box, as though it were some sort of Belgian prostitute.

Many men will bow down and accept this situation. They may even have several dogs, believing that, say, three chihuahuas is somehow equal to one Alsatian. But most of us look enviously at the men who've broken out of the spaniel trap and walk down the street with their muscly arms roped around the lead of an equally muscly dog named, aptly enough, after some German or other – Rottweiler, Doberman, that sort of thing.

But even these men are deluding themselves. Because dogs are not that dangerous. Even Dangerous dogs are not that dangerous. Any animal that can take time out from hunting you down to lick its own testicles or a lamp-post is clearly not a dedicated death machine. You wouldn't see the Terminator pause in its relentless murder quest to investigate the bum glands of another Terminator. You wouldn't be able to escape from an Alien or a Predator by throwing a bit of fillet steak laced with Anadin at it. And thus dogs are not particularly dangerous.

No, as a Dangerous Man you need to acquire a much more dangerous kind of pet. How about a big cat? By 'big cat' we don't meant an obese tabby; these are, frankly, rubbish, and if somehow you have got one by mistake you would be best off feeding it to your boa constrictor for a laugh. All regular cats are unpleasant rather than Dangerous, and any opponent which can be disarmed by catnip isn't that scary. ('Now I will kill you . . . what? What's this? Oo! I'm dancing!') And also cats are just a bit *too* nasty. There's always the danger that a cat will plot against you, or move in with the neighbours, or just tell women that you're going bald. Regular cats are to be avoided, then.

As for the proper Big Cats, from school books and David Attenborough, there are many extremely dangerous big cats, the most popular of which is the lion, whose main flaw is that it gets really tired after dinner, like your grandad. Lions are also a bit tricky in that the cool ones – known as 'lionesses', who are the ones who really do the hunting and killing and so on – are the less cool-looking ones, because they don't have those brilliant 1970s rock-singer manes, whereas the ones that do – the 'man lions' – spend most of their time asleep, like your grandad.

Tigers are pretty good but they're quite rare, and if you're seen as the sort of person who owns six tigers because they're rare you'll be confused with collectors, who tend to go in for non-Dangerous things like stamps and chutney. (Even worse are white tigers, although they seem to be allergic to con-jurors.) Leopards and cheetahs are a bit effeminate, which is cool – effeminacy, as Roman emperors and reality show winners have proven, is no bar to being Dangerous – but when your most notable attribute is being good at running, that seems show-offy rather than Dangerous. Which leaves ocelots, frankly, and, as they have hair on the tips of their ears, again we're back at the 'like your grandad' option.

There are other dangerous animals, of course – bears are pretty dangerous and will not become your friend, no matter how often you repeat their jokes on Twitter or make them

CDs of your favourite music. Snakes are bloody dangerous, because you can never remember in a room full of snakes which are the crushy ones and which are the spit in your OW I'M BLIND I'M BLIND! ones. But bears are hard to sneak home (no, putting a hat on a bear and giving it a piggyback will not fool your landlady) and if snakes are that dangerous how come they can be bested by a forked stick?

Oh, and spiders, of course. Spiders are pretty good. Voted, famously, as 'Most Horrible Thing' at the *Smash Hits* Awards for fifteen years in a row, spiders not only look terrifying but also come, brilliantly, in both 'hairy' and 'non-hairy' mode, like those enormous gay men in specialist magazines. Spiders do, however, require a lot of maintenance and, if American films are to be believed, will always escape from their expensive vivariums just as you are about to get jiggy with a beautiful, if scream-inclined, Hollywood actress. The consequences, both in real life and in movies, are never hilarious.

There is only one truly suitable really dangerous pet. It's not as big as a lion, but it's portable. It's low-maintenance, and while you can take it anywhere and nobody will notice, once you mention you've got one people will go absolutely batshit and run like hell. Also, you'd have to be slightly mad to own one, which is sort of the point. The dangerous pet in question is the virus.

Viruses come in all shapes and sizes. Some are fairly harmless, like colds and rashes. Some have big reputations, like bird flu, which threatened to devastate humanity but only really succeeded in giving some sparrows a headache. But some viruses are really, really heavy. If you could get your hands on a couple of test tubes of smallpox, you'd be laughing (unless you dropped them, in which case you'd be coughing, and choking, and crying).

And also you'd be one step nearer the Dangerous Man's number two fantasy, which is of course, being a Supervillain (number one is, of course, being a Superhero). Supervillains always require a virus to launch into an unsuspecting world. Although, for some reason, they also seem to have a cat on their lap. If they reversed this trend – having a virus on their lap and threatening to launch a cat into the world – then we'd see something.

P.S. If you find before buying this book that you have gone out and bought a lion, or a bear, or similar, don't worry. Just drive it down to your nearest moor (using a rented van, not the Porsche – claws and upholstery don't go) and release it. You don't need to pay for its upkeep and maintenance any more, and for the rest of its life you'll have the joy of seeing it in blurry photographs and mobile-phone videos sent to tabloid newspapers and Sky News.

DANGEROUS DOGS

Dangerous Dogs are so much a real thing that there's even an Act named after them. If you're the outdoor type, dangerous dogs are fantastic things to own; generally speaking they're not that dangerous to you, unless you forget to feed them. And even if you are the absent-minded type, it's one thing forgetting where you left the remote control (on top of the television) but it's quite another forgetting to feed the Rottweilers. They won't forget that they're hungry, and neither will you when you look down and see them polishing off your right foot.

So Dangerous dogs can be hard work. You have to train them. They're not chihuahuas; you can't just carry them round in a man-bag and hope your chauffeur cleans up their mess. For a start, you'd be hard pressed to get a Dobermann Pinscher in a shopping trolley, let alone a man-bag, and they ate the chauffeur weeks ago. Maybe you're just not the right kind of homeowner to have Dangerous dogs; if you haven't got a huge field to keep them in, then traditionally your only other option is a junkyard, preferably one with lots and lots of really big chains to rattle. Junkyards are good. But you possibly don't have a junk-

Rottweilers often learn basket weaving in prison.

yard or a field. You probably don't even have a garden, which would be the mininum if all you owned was a slightly bad-tempered cocker spaniel.

There is a way out of this dilemma: faking it. Danger lies in not just the reality of Danger, but also the appearance of Danger. If you get a fairly innocuous dog, even a little one, it can be made to look much more Dangerous by simply putting a muzzle on it. You'd be surprised how scary a poodle can look with a metal guard on its non-slavering jaws. And if you've only got a pug, put an eyepatch on it. Oh, and if you have a really, really small dog, get a hockey mask from an Action Man hockey player and hey presto, it's wearing the same muzzle as Sir Anthony Hopkins in *Silence of the Lambs*. Impressive!

DANGEROUS CATS

All cats are bastards. The mere ownership of a cat tells the world that at least one of you is dangerous. Just hope for your sake that onlookers think it's you.

DANGEROUS SNAKES

Pretty much the same as Dangerous Spiders, but somehow more acceptable, if only because there are two kinds of Dangerous Snake. There's the Big Fat Snake, which is dangerous because it could crush and eat you if it wanted, but to be honest it's probably stuck behind the radiator and it's full of hamsters anyway so you're safe, unless it falls on you. And then there's the Little Venomous Snake, which is a whole other thing entirely. Venomous snakes are genuinely really

'Ah-choo!'

Dangerous, because you can never remember if they're the bitey kind or the spitty kind and before you can remember it'll be too late and you'll be staggering around the room clutching your face and screaming, 'AAAARGH! Spitty kind! Spitty kind!' Which is bad news for you but hilarious for everyone else in the room.

DANGEROUS PIRANHA FISH

Why? For a start cleaning the tank is a total nightmare, as they'd eat their way through the little net, never mind your fingers. And feeding them? Oh look, they've eaten their dinner in five seconds. That's about twenty-three hamsters an hour. That's prohibitively expensive. Best way to use up your piranhas and impress visitors with your Dangerous credentials is knock the tank over, wait till the piranhas have carked it, and then serve them up for dinner. Piranha and Chips is a

An estate agent, yesterday.

sexy dinner option in anyone's book. Especially when you open it up there's a hamster.

DANGEROUS SPIDERS

Slightly irritating is how we see people who own Dangerous spiders. A bit affected, really. On the one hand, it's a Dangerous animal that can cause actual harm. On the other, why not go the whole hog and dress as Count Poncing Dracula? Why not get a bag of bats while you're at it? A rat with a little 'punk rock' wig? Poisonous spiders, unless you're an actual Asian mastercriminal or a very bad pet-shop owner indeed, are the traditional mark of a Dangerous person who is Trying Too Hard. With all due respect to Alice Cooper. Woo!

CHAPTER 24

THE UNTAMED GARDEN

*If Richard Branson had been in charge
of the Battle of Britain . . .*

ardens are safe-sounding places, the Garden of Eden being the most renowned. Then again, snake and apple. 'Come into the garden, Maud,' said Tennyson, for reasons that are now unclear but probably to do with Victorian romance. Despite this, we're with Tennyson, because the garden is a fantastic battleground for the Dangerous Middle-Aged Man. Like a suburban Rambo fighting his way through the jungles of privet round the back of his house, the Dangerous Middle-Aged Man takes his life in his hands every time he ventures out into his garden. Gardens are a way of enjoying an unsafe lifestyle without having to leave the comfort of your own domicile, and there are many ways to make an English urban garden into your own personal Vietnam.

BARBECUES

If this book were called upon to provide the defining image of the British male, it would be this: a man in shorts and a Hawaiian T-shirt standing in his garden in a thunderstorm, trying to grill sausages in the driving rain. Because while in Australia a 'barbie' conjures up images of sunshine, beer and crustaceans, and in America it's fun and sun and smoke and beers before 'the game', whatever that is, in Britain a barbecue has nothing at all to do with either pleasure or good weather. A barbecue is a challenge, purely and simply, and it is this that adds Danger to an otherwise bland dining experience.

For an added frisson of fear, you should hold an umbrella over your head as lightning streaks the sky and you cook your steaks. This will protect your guests from any sudden bolts but will also add an element of much-needed drama to your barbie. Should the weather prove clement, then use as much lighter fuel as possible when trying to set the coals on fire – there's nothing more fun for the kiddies than the sight of a man's hair bursting into flames as he tries to put it out with warm lager. And since most people will be chatting and drinking instead of concentrating on the quality of your cookery, use the cheapest cuts of meat and the ones whose use-by dates are of purely historical interest.

SHEDS

Sheds are where tools go to die. If you can't find that strimmer or those secateurs, chances are they've crawled off into the shed to spend their last days cowering sadly in a corner. Like animals, tools are at their most dangerous when they're wounded, which is almost certainly why they will attack you when you try to force your way into your shed. Sensible men counter this by putting their tools into labelled boxes or on designated hooks and hangers so that they can find implements whenever they need to. Dangerous men follow ancient instincts and just throw everything in and hope it doesn't bounce back at them. It always bounces back. And where else would you get the chance to recreate those classic silent-comedy 'flipping a rake into your face' routines than your garden shed? With careless planning, the garden shed can be turned into a death trap.

PONDS

It is said that a person can drown in six inches of water. You'd have to be face down, though. Ponds can be made more exciting by digging deeper, so that if you do fall in – and after a few drinks anything can happen – you're bound to be in danger. Why not make your pond fifty feet deep? Or fill it with something a bit more exciting than a few shubunkins and a carp. Why not get some pike and some toxic pondweed? A few biting and stinging insects might make a nice change from the ubiquitous water-boatman, and of course there's that old standby the piranha fish. Any of these can be obtained via the internet, and would make a thrilling addition to any garden pond. Water snakes are good too, as they can be mistaken for pondweed – with hilarious consequences!

BIG MOTOR MOWERS

Everyone who is anyone knows the story of country singer George Jones whose drinking got so out of hand that, legend has it, his wife Tammy Wynette hid his car keys to stop

The Thousand Year Allotment takes shape.

him going into town to buy more liquor. George, with all the natural cunning of the boozer, simply drove into town on his lawnmower (said mower presumably being one of those big American ones and not a pushable British one, which would take ages). This is the sort of thinking that only a truly Dangerous Middle-Aged Man could come up with, as it combines so many kinds of risk – alcohol abuse, reckless driving, and a streak of logical insanity. Big motor mowers are also fun to combine with drinking as you may fall under yours and become clippings.

CHAPTER 25

DANGER MONEY

Money is a very Dangerous thing. If you haven't got any, you may well die. If you haven't got a lot, you'll become stressed. And if you have a lot, you'll wear yourself out trying to make sure that nobody else gets their hands on it. The only non-Dangerous financial option is to have so much that it all becomes meaningless and you can just go about the place giving it away (but even this angers some people who will try and get it off you on the grounds that clearly you can't be trusted with the stuff).

At your time of life, also, you should be able to look both ways, at your presumably dissolute past, where you spent every penny that came in on wine, women and Wii tennis, and at your wobbly future, which may see you eating sandwiches from rubbish bins and writing begging letters to people you think you might have been at school with. But this is *The Dangerous Book for Middle-Aged Men*. We're not particularly interested in financial prudence or that 'planning for the future' nonsense.

Remember the parable about the ant and the grasshopper? The ant had a miserable time all summer storing up food for the winter, while the grasshopper just dicked about having a fantastic summer generally doing sod all. The parable tells us, with the sadistic thrill of a friendless spinster carrying a hot basket of malicious gossip, that the ant was able to survive the winter with its store of ant food, while the grasshopper died screaming in the cold and serve it right for enjoying itself.

This is drivel. Experience tells us that in reality the ant put all its food into a Safe Ant-food Account, but a bank used all the ant food to invest in a failed venture capital scheme, leaving the ant foodless and broke. Meanwhile the grasshopper made a funny video of itself dicking about to a rap tune and put it on YouTube and got a million hits, which led to its own show on MTV. It gave the ant a job as a runner, which was kind but indirectly caused the ant to become a cocaine addict.

The true moral of the story? Don't copy ants. And take a look if you will at this Dangerous Guide to Finance.

PROPERTY

This used to be the bedrock of all safe investment. Buy a house, we were all told, and you'll always have money, because there isn't going to be any more land and property never goes down in value. This is an entirely true maxim, except for the several times when it has been entirely untrue. People are always buying houses in the belief that their value will just keep going up and up, and then expressing surprise when the property market crashes and they find themselves with negative equity. Similarly, people waiting to sell property in a recession have a tendency to wait for the slump to 'bottom out', which it will, but not until their home has reached a value so minuscule that it will never be worth more than the cost of a broken rocking horse again.

Property is not only risky, it is a dull investment. Add spice and be a Dangerous investor by using what everyone knows is the best indicator of the property market – the Monopoly board. Go down the Old Kent Road and offer someone £60 for their house. These days the markets are so bad you might just get away with it. In fact, run your entire financial life according to Monopoly. Drawing cards from Chance and the Community Chest is just as good a way of dealing with your investments as any, and means that you don't have to buy the *Financial Times*, which is good, because any newspaper that's printed on pink paper can't be expected to be taken that seriously. Demand ten pounds from your friends and if they query it show them the card that says it's your birthday. Email the organisers of beauty contests and insist they give you your £100 prize. And go down Oxford Street and charge rent to tourists who are staying in one of 'your' hotels. If they are sufficiently American, they may find this quaint and hand over the £560.

BUY TO LET

This is notably one of the worst investments you can make, because not only are you as much at the mercy of the market as any other homeowner, but also you have little or no control over the people who live in your property or properties. You buy a perfectly nice slum, do it up with a lick of paint and a bit of Cif sprayed into the cooker, and suddenly you have a property for which you can charge in rent per week about five times what you actually paid for it. But are your new tenants grateful? No. They keep phoning you up (why did you give them your real phone number?) and demanding that you fix the water and the leaking ceiling, when it seems perfectly clear to you that the water is the cause of the leaking ceiling, and if everyone would just leave well alone it would be fine. And then the words 'slum landlord' are bandied about when all you were trying to do was help some people.

On the plus side, there is a Dangerous feeling of power and excitement as you walk down the road, eyeing up your crumbling tenements, laughing and twirling your imaginary moustachios while you watch elderly tenants fall through rotting planks into the basement. If you're really lucky you might get to be on *Panorama*, and then proper rich slum landlords and gangsters will befriend you, and you can sit on their yachts twirling your moustachios and drinking Krug from a poor old lady's bonnet.

PENSIONS

Pensions are Dangerous things whichever way you look at it. On the one hand, if you don't have one you're not signing up for security and happiness. On the other hand – who wouldn't want to give away a fairly large sum from their income every month, at a time in their life when they can't really afford it, to a faceless multinational ill-regulated bank who will use the money to shore up its own mistakes and then, if it doesn't actually go bust before you retire, will gracelessly give you back your own money, which thanks to inflation is now worth about 50 per cent of what it was when you first paid it in? What could be safer than relying on businessmen for your future? At least with the poorhouse there was a duty of care. Even Mister Bumble didn't charge you £400 a month for the privilege of spending your money on Victorian tarts and then, when you needed the dosh, feign bankruptcy or fall off the side of a boat into the Mediterranean.

If you are going to involve yourself with a pension scheme, don't subscribe to one – set one up. The qualifications for doing so seem fairly minimal, and if you're worried that you don't have an actual bank or building society behind you, don't be – you could probably pick up HSBC for a few bob these days, never mind revive the name of a long-lost company like Bradford and Bingley or the Prudential.

SHARES

Remember – the value of shares can go up as well as down. Something to think about as you sit at home at your computer, head in hands, watching your so-called 'portfolio' sink like a fat man in a diving suit to the bottom of the FTSE. Your equally absurdly-named 'basket' of shares is no longer giving you a dividend; in fact, things are so bad that the companies are ringing you up to ask if they can have their money back.

Shares are like anything: when the sun is shining they are brilliant, but when things are bad – which is most of the time – they are useless. If you want to give your money to people you've never met to buy not actual wheat or water or heat or even pictures of wheat or water or heat but pieces of paper which mention wheat or water or heat, then fair enough. You'd be better off buying pieces of silver paper because at least they're shiny and when you lick them you get a funny tingle.

The Dangerous Middle-Aged Man loves shares. He cannot resist running onto the floor of any stock market and shouting 'Buy! Sell! Buy! Sell!' at panicky-looking young cockneys and cocaine-addled City boys, thereby causing the

'Oh no, we've lost millions of pounds of other people's money. Damn! We might get smaller bonuses this year.'

world's economy to collapse save for the ten shares he bought in a factory that makes anti-panic pills in Taiwan. He will take any old punt from a friend of a friend who heard a rumour from a taxi driver. He will plough his savings into Rio Tinto Zinc even though he doesn't know what it is. And who knows, he may even become Dangerously rich.

ART

Ah, the credit crunch. So named, presumably, because it crunches its way through all your money and property and investments like a sort of financial termite, chewing away at stocks and shares like there is no tomorrow, which for many people in the City there isn't. One thing about the most recent bout of money trouble is the way it has affected almost every aspect of the money world. Until recently, for example, the area that always seemed to be free of depression or recession in times of financial crisis was art, the reasoning presumably being that a) works of art are so weird and unfathomable that how the hell do we know if they've lost value anyway and b) the chances of Rembrandt coming back from the dead are fairly slender (and no doubt Sotheby's are keeping an eye on DNA research to make sure that this never happens).

Art is also traditionally a good investment because, basically, only rich people can afford it and rich people are not the sort of folk who tend to invest in things which won't make them money. But this time round a strange thing happened. Major art auctions – which are the equivalent of car-boot sales for very rich people – started to run into trouble. Pieces old – like Picasso – and new – like Damien Hurst, weren't reaching their reserve prices, and were being removed from the sale by sulky auction houses.

This is relevant to the Dangerous Middle-Aged Man, because if you are in a reckless mood and you should be at your time of life then now is the time to get some art. Ignore the disdain of your children and the panic in the eyes of your partner as with one hand you check out second- and even third-mortgage deals on the internet and with the other you phone up art dealers and ask them how much a nice Francis Bacon is going for these days. We may be talking a million pounds or so, but if you can raise it – perhaps selling a few organs here and there, maybe volunteering for a few medical experiments involving gene splicing – then in a few years' time you'll be incredibly rich. Risky, perhaps, but that's the point.

LOTTERY TICKETS

They're a fun investment, aren't they? A pound a week guaranteeing you a few minutes' excitement on a Saturday night and the chance to become extremely rich without doing any work or having to marry a horse-faced girl. All right, so maybe you can end up spending more than a pound a week, but it's better for you than drinking and statistically everyone is going to win a few bob at some time or other. It's not, however, the losing that's the Dangerous part of doing the Lottery. It's the winning. Because while your life is unlikely to be unaffected by you not winning the Lottery, it almost certainly is going to be changed totally if you win the bloody thing. And as far as we can tell there are very few examples of people winning it and continuing to be sane and happy.

Here's the scenario: before you win the Lottery, your life is as glum or as pleasant as anyone else's. You have average pleasures, average vices and average problems. Your character is by and large impeccable. You probably don't do anything weird. The moment that you win the Lottery, though, you change completely. You suddenly develop the urge not only to take all your friends, relatives, acquaintances and newly acquired hangers-on to the pub and buy them a drink, but you have to do so in the manner of a footballer on a night out in Liverpool, hectoring strangers, getting into fights, throwing glasses and ending up being barred from a pub that you first went to with your dad when you were 17.

You used to drive the one car, a Ford – something that was fine for you and the family. You would park it in your garage or in your drive. You would use it to take the kids to school, go to work, and occasionally pick up your partner from the station when she'd been to visit her mother. Now you are seized by a terrible compulsion to buy at least eight cars, all of which have ludicrous spoilers and Day-Glo bits and chrome wheels. You park them on your lawn, and do so at fifty miles an hour, only managing to prevent yourself from crashing into your own front room by doing a massive swerve at the last minute. You let your friends drive them too, so that when you all get back from the pub you can get out of the cars at the same time, slamming doors and shouting each others' names in case you've all forgotten who you are. Meanwhile the kids are still waiting outside their school and your partner has gone back to her mother's.

And this pervades every aspect of your life. You become a yahoo, a lout, an oik and, eventually, an ASBO. It's a sad decline from your formerly decorous past, but one day you'll wake up and see your reflection in the bottom of a glass of WKD, a bloated, middle-aged gold-chain-wearing oaf. The only consolation here is that soon the money will run out, your friends will be just as quickly diminished, and you will return to something approaching your old life, except your wife and kids will have left you and you won't be able to get a job.

There are, as we noted, some people whose lives aren't changed by winning the Lottery. They live in the same houses as before, go to the same pubs and take the same holidays as they did, and even keep their old jobs. But where's the Danger in that?

(HAPTER 26

DANGEROUSLY RICH & POOR

Being rich is a very good way to lead the Dangerous life. But if you can't be rich, then working for the rich is also quite Dangerous. This is largely because rich people are often not very nice, and have no regard for human life save their own. Years of being waited on hand and foot and owning most of the world make rich people see the rest of humanity as interchangeable and replaceable items. But even rich people need other poorer people to do jobs for them, and as a Dangerous Man this is where you come in.

MANSERVANT

A horrible job. Even butlers who are the top end of servant-ing have a rotten life. Look at Jeeves, people say. He essentially runs Bertie Wooster as though he were a small country for the same wages as a McDonald's manager and he goes to all the posh places Bertie Wooster does, except he has to eat in the kitchen and sleep under the stairs. And that's at the top end. Most servants spend their lives fetching and carrying all day and are only invited to give their opinion as proof of how stupid the common man is. You'll end up marrying the cook and you will die without anyone ever knowing your first name. Also there is the fact that in wartime you'll be expected to join up with your owner and do your bit, which in your case will mean being blown up as you bring sandwiches and champagne to the officers.

GAMEKEEPER

One of the best Dangerous jobs. You get to chase poachers, most of whom are armed. You get to hang out with wild animals, some of which may attack you. And you get to sleep with Lady Chatterley. Sadly you are no longer allowed to set mantraps, but we're sure that if you're discreet about it you could put out the odd one here and there.

It's easier to shoot birds when they're already on the washing line.

PERSONAL ASTROLOGER

Despite their lives being completely predictable – they're rich so they'll probably live for a very long time and enjoy their lives – rich people are inordinately fond of hiring personal astrologers. Partly this is because they're all paranoid and think someone is out to get them, and thus hire astrologers as a kind of early-warning system. And partly it's because they like being told how brilliant they are and how much extra money and jewels are coming their way. If you do your job properly, it is a very Dangerous one: i.e. if you can predict the future, and you tell them that they're going to get mumps or lose their money, they'll have you shot. Also if you're bad at it and they do become the victims of a botched assassination attempt, they'll be furious that you didn't tell them about it and have you shot. The only almost safe way of doing this job is to just make it up. Tell them how rich they're going to be and how they're going to live for ever and just hope it all comes true. Since they're already rich, it almost certainly will.

FOOL OR JESTER

A ridiculous job because first of all you have to be really funny, but in a weird, incomprehensible medieval way. Fools say things like 'What la? A capon?' and then everyone waits to see what the king will do and if he laughs you're fine, but you don't really know what he's laughing at. And if he doesn't laugh you will be executed, which is a bit unfair when you look at what's on Channel Four these days. You're also – and this is the really Dangerous part – expected to remind the king that he is only human by doing jokes *about him*. How can

Robbie Williams, on the road again.

this be safe? Kings are notoriously egotistical people. Having a king say to you, 'Go on, fool, take the mickey out of me. I, Charles the Bloody, totally don't mind', is like being gored on the horns of a dilemma.

FOOD TASTER

Less common now, what with prepackaged food, but clearly a Dangerous job. The only safe way to do it is to say to your employer, 'Look, how about you cook tonight?' Although he might be a cannibal as so many crazy dictators are. Still, eating someone's uncle is slightly preferable to being poisoned, we expect.

TOYBOY

Being a Dangerous Middle-Aged Man does not preclude you from being the younger lover of a rich woman (or man). It just means that your paramour is going to be incredibly old, which works in your favour as you may well outlive them and inherit the gold and diamonds. The Danger, of course, is that you'll be going out with a really old person and your friends will laugh at you, until you inherit the gold and diamonds.

DANGEROUSLY POOR

Poverty is no bar to Danger – in fact, it's a positive asset as most poor people will confirm. Having no money adds an element of risk to one's life. But it's not all starving to death and feeling unhappy; thanks to this book, you can live a Dangerously Poor life. Here are some tips:

LIVING ON THE STREET

Homelessness is very much not good for you. But if you've been through a bad divorce and the wife's got everything, why not try the street? There's lots to do and people to meet. Not much effort is involved as you can either sit down with a piece of cardboard and beg, or stand up and sell copies of the *Big Issue*. Drugs and alcohol are freely available, so in many ways it's like being in a rock band except you don't have to play any concerts. And on the days you get to see the kids, use the cute little one to boost your begging returns. Not only will you make more money, your children will learn about finance at the sharp end. Everybody wins.

SQUATTING

Not as popular as it used to be, but sure to be on the upturn as the recession worsens, squatting is actually a lot of fun. First of all, you get to be a burglar as you break into a house (we recommend breaking into the nicest house you can find because everyone likes comfort and there'll be more furniture to burn). Then get some friends round because everyone likes company. And finally, just hang out. What are the Dangers of squatting? Well, you probably won't have any hot water or heat or light, so essentially you're living in a very nice hut. You'll eventually run out of furniture to chop up for firewood, and your room-mates are almost certainly going to be really annoying self-righteous dope smokers. Oh, and you're liable to get attacked by the actual owners if they fail to take the legal route. They may even use dogs.

TRAMP FIGHTING

This is an appalling practice invented by American college kids, who call it 'bum fighting', which makes it sound even worse. People pay tramps to fight each other, basically. It's very barbaric but if you're desperate it's a way to earn money. Also if you do enough fights and win enough money you can pay some American college kids to fight each other to the death.

HERMITING

Hermits are supposed to be really cool because they live in caves and don't talk. Well, bears do that and nobody ever calls them cool. Being a hermit has its advantages. You get plenty of 'you time' and people who think you're cool bring you food and drink in exchange for them asking you questions and you giving them incomprehensible answers. The main dangers of being a hermit are going mad from loneliness and being attacked by the bears that also live in your cave. Also some hermits spend their lives sitting on top of a big pole and you're not telling us THAT'S not dangerous.

TRAVELLING

Remember 'travellers'? That was the official term for what most people called 'crusties' and your mum and dad call 'spongers'. Travellers were like the military wing of the gypsies, in that, like gypsies, they roamed the land and made do, except they didn't do it in quaint little caravans pulled by horses, they did it in ambulances painted khaki and ex-Army vehicles. Travellers also believed in their ancient right to get into Glastonbury for free, which for many of them seemed to be the sole purpose of being a traveller, and in fact when this right was revoked by Glastonbury boss Michael Eavis in the 1980s the heart went out of the travelling movement and they all got jobs and bought houses and paid for their Glastonbury tickets like everyone else.

Travelling now is dangerous, because in the old days travellers had convoys but these days it will just be you in your ambulance painted khaki and the Devon and Cornwall constabulary will descend on you like the wolf upon the fold. You are a fugitive, and a smelly one at that.

PICKPOCKET

Obviously a Dangerous job, because it's illegal and highly risky. Not only do you have to be good at it, but these days wallets contain credit cards with PIN numbers and very little cash. So essentially the modern pickpocket is someone who collects wallets, which have very little resale value.

'FIND THE LADY' MEN

This old dodge is still going, and is quite Dangerous because it's illegal and also because it's easy to make the fundamental mistake of forgetting to put the 'lady' in your pocket. Playing Find The Lady and having twenty-four people go 'There she is!' will cost you a lot of money.

CHAPTER 27

DANGER AT AUCTION

The internet auction is discussed elsewhere because it's not a real auction. Real auctions are far more pulse-racingly scary because they take place in real time in real rooms with real people and a real man with a real hammer who so far as you can tell behind your coating of sweat and terror is saying, 'Whadamabadamanyabadamafivehunnersixhunnersenhunner thousanatwothousanathreefourfivesixthousanaSOLD!' and everyone is looking at you. Yes, auctions are properly Dangerous. They also do not lack variety, which is no bad thing, as you can buy anything at an auction. You can buy a little pen. You can buy a pig. You can buy a house. The sky is effectively the limit so far as auctions go, which is why they are so Dangerous.

Consider for a moment the difference between auctions – Dangerous – and shopping – less so. Shopping can be stressful but all the prices are written on stuff and there is no sense of competition. If someone else buys the thing that you want, then they will probably have some more of that thing in stock. Nobody is shouting at you. Nobody is waving their arms and making the prices go up. It's relatively sedate. Auctions are not sedate. They are weird. To the viewer, it's one man on a stage going, 'Wabadadabada wabadadabada gomegomeGOB!' with some people at the back scratching their heads mysteriously but to you, sitting in the middle actually wanting to bid on something, it's utterly terrifying. And not for the faint of heart – so join us now as we take you through a few tips on how to make auctions even more Dangerous.

'Lot 25, another bloody painting . . .'

POSH AUCTIONS

We've all seen the feeble auctions they have on the television in the afternoon, where people go and bid for old teddy bears or three-legged milking stools. There's no point going to any of them. No, the sort of auction you want to attend is the kind where items like Fabergé eggs or Gutenberg Bibles are hauled onto the stage and where if you so much as close one eye the wrong way, the auctioneer shouts 'SOLD! to the middle-aged man who closed his eye the wrong way!' You've got to be careful or, rather, reckless in these situations. If you're going to bid for something you can't really afford, then bid for something you REALLY can't really afford, like a Rolls-Royce Silver Ghost, or Narnia.

CHARITY AUCTIONS

These are incredibly Dangerous. You turn up to a charity auction to help a friend swell the numbers. You offer to help drive up the bids by putting in a few early ones yourself, and then feel a chill as you realise that your early bid is in fact the only bid for the signed Hull Kingston Rovers shirt that you have somehow offered four thousand pounds for. You take it home and hide it in a drawer, planning to sell it on eBay for a fraction of what you paid, but even this plan is thwarted when your wife washes it and the rare-ish autographs all come off.

BIDDING

Bidding is, as we've seen, a skill. It's not simply a matter of saying, 'Yes, I'd like that, please' every time something comes up for auction. There is a skilled language of nuance involved. At the back of the room are the telephone bidders, whose representatives talk quietly into mobiles and nod at the auctioneer. In the middle are the old hands, who might tap a programme against their head or just wave a languid hand. And at the front there's you, going, 'Ooh! Ooh! OOH!' and wriggling like you need the toilet. Why? Because it's more exciting that way and if you keep up a constant stream of neurotic fidgeting you'll help to push the prices up, and even if you don't win the item you were bidding for you'll ensure that some poor rich sod has had to pay about £15,000 more than he wanted for that little ormolu carriage clock. In fact, just to make sure the prices rocket up even further, why not take along a friend – preferably someone with a nervous tic, or at least prone to sudden movements. At best you'll have a fun afternoon and the knowledge that you nearly owned a Van Eyck. At worst? Well, just make sure all the fire exits are unlocked before you sit down.

BEING AN AUCTIONEER

Very few people have such power over mankind as auction-eers. It's not a coincidence that they have the same little hammers that judges do - because auctioneers preside over everyone in the room and with one tap can sentence you to a life sentence of poverty and debt. So why not pretend to be one? Imagine the excitement and novelty of taking the stage, gavel in hand, and firstly making up your own descriptions of the items – 'Lot 42, not in the catalogue, a dressing table that belonged to Captain Kirk, very rare, the drawers have been stuffed with rubies at the request of the previous owner, shall we start the bidding at £400,000?' – and then 'accepting' bids by looking at people who aren't even paying attention and saying, 'Lady in the pink hat, £400,000, any advance, man texting by the window, £500,000' and so on. It's not even that Dangerous because by the time the man texting by the window has explained that he hasn't got half a million pounds and he was only texting his girlfriend to tell her that he was at a completely mental auction, you're through the fire exit and out of there.

CHAPTER 28

DANGEROUS FAITH

Religion is traditionally a very Dangerous thing. From the early Christian martyrs, thrown to the lions for their beliefs, to the heretic burned at the stake and the thousands killed in religious wars over the centuries, the whole business has lacked any semblance of calm and sanity, thereby making it perfect for the Dangerous Middle-Aged Man.

WALKING OVER HOT COALS

There are strict health and safety rules about doing this, obviously, so if you're a London resident please make sure the coals are smokeless. The best way to approach the task is to meditate while walking. If you can't meditate, try drinking heavily. If you have limited space, one of those mini-barbecues is ideal as you can light it and just walk up and down on the spot.

You'll never fall asleep at the wheel again.

LYING ON A BED OF NAILS

Popular in India with middle-aged mystics, although we're not entirely sure if they do it because they like nails or they just have their beds the wrong way round. You might want to get some practice in first by staying the night at a Premier Inn. For added Danger, you could combine your night on a bed of nails by practising selections from the Kama Sutra, also popular in India.

GOING ON A CRUSADE

Crusades are one of the most powerfully futile inventions in the history of history. Designed allegedly for the removal of Jerusalem from Arab hands, they basically ensured that a constant flow of the flower of English chivalry and the bulk of English peasantry was ebbing into the Middle East, never to return. The most absurd crusade was of course the Children's Crusade, which never stood a chance.

Starting a crusade is still possible today, as the continuing religious wars and exhortations to Jihad or 'holy war' indicate. It's hard for us to recommend a faith for the Dangerous Middle-Aged Man to join from which to foment a crusade but our money's on the Scientologists, because they are the maddest.

BEING A HASHASIN

These legendary killers gave us the word 'assassin'. It's not known if they're still going but there was one in a Dan Brown novel so it must be true. Being a Hashasin is more Dangerous than being an assassin, as the latter is a highly trained killing machine who moves anonymously through crowds with his high-powered rifle hidden in a case, while the former is a drugged-up nutter who goes round dressed like an unemployed genie.

BEING A HERETIC

Religions are all founded on various degrees of tolerance and enlightenment, but only for the people in them. If you have become dissatisfied with your religion and become tempted by some slight variation on it, like Manicheanism or snake-handling, your religious leaders will come down on you like a ton of bricks. Be prepared to undergo horrific tortures and pointless, painful interrogation.

BEING A RELIGIOUS FUNDAMENTALIST

Arguably being a religious fundamentalist is more danger-ous for the people around you than it is for yourself. Religious fundamentalism can be Dangerous in other ways too. Your social life will shrink to a nubbin, as the only people prepared to hang out with you will be other religious fundamentalists. You'll find your life is proscribed by hundreds of weird rules, from not being allowed zips and not eating meat on a Friday to strapping a bomb to your chest and walking into a crowded shop. And worst of all, you'll probably go to hell for being a complete idiot.

BEING A BIT RELIGIOUS IN A VAGUE WAY

This used to be fine, and is the very essence of the Church of England, a church designed specifically to appeal to people who sort of, well, believe in God but don't like to go on about it. Unfortunately, since the invention of Richard Dawkins and his annoying hectoring egomaniacal books, people with vague religious beliefs are constantly being hectored and harassed and accused of bombing abortion clinics. It is now actually Dangerous to sort of be thinking about getting your kids baptised as if you do a load of atheist nutters will turn up and call you an evil Church of England bastard.

BEING AN ATHEIST

Because if you're wrong, you'll burn.

CHAPTER 29

DANGERSTALGIA

The past, it has been claimed, is a foreign country. We interpret this to mean that the past, like a foreign country, is a horrible place to visit, full of risk and terror, where places that you thought would be fun to see are not at all how you thought they'd be. The past, then, is not much like Switzerland. Which is a good thing, because who wants to go to Switzerland when you can go to somewhere much more Dangerous and exciting?

The past is fraught with thrills because, for a kick-off, you can never really go back. Angus Young, the guitarist with AC/DC, knows this full well when each night he unwillingly dresses up as a schoolboy complete with shorts, blazer and cape, each time looking like a portrait of the young yet hideously shrivelled Dorian Gray. Ageing gigolos in singles bars know this as every night they stuff themselves into suits that John Travolta would have scorned in *Saturday Night Fever*. And the Dangerous Middle–Aged Man knows this, but the difference is, he doesn't care. If the past is a foreign country, then he refuses to acknowledge any borders. Because life, like the TARDIS, is bigger on the inside than on the outside. Come back with us now as we list a few of the more fun Dangerous aspects of Going Back.

COWBOYS AND INDIANS

And other games which kids these days probably don't play, because which is more fun, running round in a cardboard hat pointing your fingers and going P-CHOW! or driving around an estate in a stolen car with a real gun? We say the former, although nowadays this in itself is Dangerous, because the sight of a small posse of middle-aged men pretending to ride horses round the park while going P-CHOW! and rolling around in the grass would worry the pants off Social Services, never mind Sitting Bull. Still, if you're of that generation, or one that played Commandos and Germans, or any war-related game, there's still a lot of mileage in that sort of thing. Especially now that you're about the same age as John Wayne was when he made those films. Go crazy; if you've got a birthday with a 0 at the end coming up, hire a bit of a theme park where they've got a Wild West street and spend the day re-enacting gunfights. Clint Eastwood did it all his life and nobody ever said he was a pillock.

SWINGS AND ROUNDABOUTS

The park! Of course, for middle-aged men this is something of a no-go area. But if you've got kids, or you know some-one who'd be glad to get rid of them for a few hours, then you shall go to the park. But don't just sit on the bench like a nonce, get out there and use this rare opportunity to check out the facilities. Parks were great when you were nine – why should things be any different over a quarter of a century later? Because building standards are stricter nowadays, that's why, and where's the fun in that? When you were nine you could get on the slide or the swing, safe in the knowledge that there was at least fifty per cent chance of falling off and breaking your neck. However, there is good news for the Middle-Aged Man. Nowadays you are about ten stone heavier. This makes for Dangerous fun, as you could actually break the slide, smash up the swings, and cause the round-about to roll across the park like a giant killer cheese. And don't even THINK of sitting on the plastic elephant on springs.

GO-KARTING

There are two kinds, you know. One is the old-school sort where you make your own out of soapboxes, whatever they are, and pram wheels. They are rickety and dangerous and the centrepiece of *Rex Milligan's Busy Term* by Anthony

Whee!

Buckeridge, which remains a useful guidebook for Dangerous Middle-Aged Men if you can find a copy. However, this kind of go-kart requires both a degree of construction skill and a driver who weighs about the same as the usual contents of a normal soapbox (several bars of soap, probably), so driving one of these might prove fatal as well as nostalgic.

The other kind of go-karting is more practical, and just as Dangerous in its own way. It's the modern sort, where you drive little lawnmower-engined karts around a track covered in tyres. Not only is it just as risky as the other sort but also it can lead to world fame and recognition. This is the place where Lewis Hamilton started out. Of course, he was nine when he started, but you're a quick study, you'll catch up. Unless you break your neck first.

AVIATION

Not your big modern metal planes but your old monoplanes. Louis Bleriot crossed the Channel in what was effectively a pram with some sheets draped over wooden frames on the sides. Recent attempts to duplicate his flight, by the way, were slower – so why not trump the French by sticking a rocket engine on your plane? You could shoot from Dieppe to a burning haystack in Surrey in under twenty minutes.

CONKERS

Happy days and golden autumn afternoons spent submerging conkers in jars of vinegar and threading them. Contests on the football pitch that ended in tears as an older boy smashed the gubbins out of your conker and everyone laughed. Well, no longer. Not only is conkers banned in some schools (if you ha ha ha believe the ho ho ho newspapers), but also now that you are a big strapping lad with access to technology and money, conkers is your bitch. Get a scientist friend to implant a ball-bearing in the middle of your conker. Dip it in a powerful varnish perfected by NASA for use on the space shuttle. Use aerodynamically tested tennis-racquet strings to hold it up. And then burst into tears as a much younger boy smashes the gubbins out of your conker and everyone laughs.

Conkers.
The English equivalent
of the Prussian duel.

CAMPING

Did you camp as a child? With family, perhaps, or the Cubs? It seems possible because men of a certain age are just old enough to remember the days when going abroad was something you only did if you were in the Armed Forces. Nowadays we're all supposed to be staying at home again and saving money because of the recession, but tell that to the long-suffering people of Ayia Napa and Gran Canaria. Camping still retains something of its eccentric side, especially since actually buying a complete set of camping equipment

Keep telling yourself you're having fun . . .

is almost as dear as buying a house. There's also the absurd luxury end of camping, where you hire a yurt, which used to be a rough Mongolian herdsman's abode but is now a sort of trendy flat made out of canvas and carpets.

Nevertheless, if it's done properly, camping can be very Dangerous. The trick is to go totally roots. Instead of wasting hundreds of pounds on jet pumps and modern twist'n'throw tents and the like, go on the attack and find your dad's moth-eaten old teepee. Yes, he had one; and if he didn't, there will be some sort of horrific canvas atrocity thrown out by the local Sea Scouts. Either way, it'll be easy to find; the smell of mothballs and old sails will guide you.

Head for the country. Find a suitable campsite, preferably one with no shower facilities or standpipe. You're going native. What a shame you forgot to bring any wet wipes or bottled water. Then again, who do you think you are, the President of France? Pitch your tent. Actually, don't; it can wait. And it's perfectly safe where it is: the smell coming off it alone would deter vampires, never mind thieves. Now you need supplies. A proper camper lived off the land and scrounged eggs, butter and milk from a local farmer. Try that nowadays: the farmer is probably in London lobbying for an increase in his EU subsidy and if he does come to the door he's more likely to shoot you for trespassing.

Returning to your tent empty-handed and empty-bellied, you notice it's got dark and it's starting to rain. As you begin to pitch the tent, you also notice that most of the pegs are missing, as is a very large patch of canvas which once would have covered your head. Finally, as lightning flickers across the night sky, you go to sleep in what is essentially a huge canvas bucket. As it begins to fill with rain, reflect on this. Not only have you shown true pioneer spirit, but tomorrow when the rescue team finds you, you'll be spending two lovely weeks in a nice warm hospital bed.

EXTREME CAMPING

You can do this the hard way – you can emulate the omnivore Ray Mears and camp under a sheet of A4 paper in a rocky valley and live off grubs and things that sleep under stones. Or you can do it the less-hard way, like TV presenter Edward Michael 'Bear' Grylls, who likes to go on rough, tough hard-man expeditions for the camera, but spent his down-time in lovely, nice, soft girlie hotels. We recommend the latter, for the minibar.

Well, if we ever go to war with seventeenth-century France, we'll be fine.

HISTORICAL RECREATIONS

Those who do not learn from history are condemned to repeat it. So we are told, anyway. One group of people who are definitely condemned to repeat history are The Sealed Knot, who spend their weekends dressing as Cavaliers and Roundheads and pretending to fight each other in a field while a man does a running commentary through a PA system (which doesn't seem terrifically historically true to the period). One doubts very much that the reason Charles I lost the Battle of Marston Moor was because he was put off by a commentator with a nasal voice saying, 'Ohhh, and the Earl of Huckmore is down! That *will* be a blow for the Royalist side'.

You can add a deal of much-needed spice and Danger to these and similar events by bringing in real weapons. The pretend Oliver Cromwell won't be expecting you to pull out a Colt 45 just as he's about to accept Charles's surrender, and he certainly won't be best pleased when you make him do a dance in his underwear through Marston town centre singing 'Oliver's Army' at the top of his voice. Best of all, never mind your actual fake battles. Try and wangle your way into the Confederate Air Force, the no-way-pro-slavery-named group in the USA who fly vintage warplanes. Refight World War Two by fitting your Spitfire with real machine guns, knocking a few Mustangs out of the sky and shouting, 'Ha! Take that, FDR! This time the British properly win!'

Should this prove too expensive, we recommend that as a fully paid-up Dangerous Middle-Aged Man, you take the plunge and apply the concept of the Historical Recreation Society to other aspects of life, such as The First Day At School Recreation Society, where grown men get to alter history and flush Alan Thompson's head down the toilet instead. Or The Julie Potter's Eighteenth Birthday Party Recreation Society where this time you get off with Julie Potter, and Alan Thompson, once again, has his head flushed down the toilet.

PRETENDING TO BE FROM A DIFFERENT ERA

Given that a) pretty soon someone's going to invent an actual time machine and b) most children these days probably think Doctor Who is real, we recommend that you have a bit of Dangerous history-related fun by buying yourself a silver suit and walking up to people in the street pretending that you are from a different era. A few good things to try are: asking people what time it is, and when they say it's half past two, say in an urgent yet annoyed voice, 'No, the year, man, the YEAR!' Point at something modern that they're holding and ask them what it is and when they say it's a mobile phone, shout, 'The fools! They finally did it!' And, as a climax before somebody punches you or the police turn up, just ask them something like who is the governor of California or if they know what Simon Cowell does for a living in this 'reality'. Then, when they tell you, look downcast, say, 'Then I'm too late,' and walk slowly away.